Go with God

ATELIER: ETHNOGRAPHIC INQUIRY IN THE TWENTY-FIRST CENTURY

Kevin Lewis O'Neill, Series Editor

Go with God

POLITICAL EXHAUSTION AND EVANGELICAL POSSIBILITY IN SUBURBAN BRAZIL

Laurie Denyer Willis

UNIVERSITY OF CALIFORNIA PRESS

University of California Press
Oakland, California

© 2023 by Laurie Denyer Willis

Library of Congress Cataloging-in-Publication Data

Names: Denyer Willis, Laurie, 1983– author.
Title: Go with god : political exhaustion and evangelical possibility in
    suburban Brazil / Laurie Denyer Willis.
Other titles: Atelier (Oakland, Calif.) ; 12.
Description: Oakland, California : University of California Press, [2023] |
    Series: Atelier. Ethnographic inquiry in the twenty-first century ; 12 |
    Includes bibliographical references and index.
Identifiers: LCCN 2023006001 (print) | LCCN 2023006002 (ebook) |
    ISBN 9780520394773 (cloth) | ISBN 9780520394797 (paperback) |
    ISBN 9780520394803 (ebook)
Subjects: LCSH: Evangelicalism—Brazil—Rio de Janeiro. |
    Christianity—Brazil—Rio de Janeiro. | Equality—Brazil—Rio de
    Janeiro. | Violence—Brazil—Rio de Janeiro.
Classification: LCC BR1642.B6 D46 2023 (print) | LCC BR1642.B6 (ebook) |
    DDC 278.1/53—dc23/eng/20230614
LC record available at https://lccn.loc.gov/2023006001
LC ebook record available at https://lccn.loc.gov/2023006002

32   31   30   29   28   27   26   25   24   23
10   9   8   7   6   5   4   3   2   1

To my mum and dad

Contents

Acknowledgments

This acknowledgment cannot start anywhere but with a sincere thank you to the community of Batan and to the people who invited me in, reoriented my thinking, and insisted on—and continually demonstrated—an ethics of care that I still strive for. They pushed me, corrected me when I was wrong, and urged me to think and feel differently about the city, faith, and possibility. They gave me grace, and I hope to return it.

There is a large group of scholars who made my time in the cities of Rio and São Paulo so enriching. Thank you to Nicole Rosner, Yanilda González, Michael Wolfe, Craig Schuetze, Nick Barnes, Simone Gomes, Julia Sakr Tierney, and Peter Klein. In Rio the friendship and scholarship of Theresa Williamson, Stephanie Savell, and Erica Robb Larkins were, and continue to be, critical to my research and understanding of Rio but also to my survival as an academic and mother. They are role models in the best possible sense: each of them embodies an intelligence that is kind, open, and humane. Also in Rio I had the great privilege of being a visiting student at the Pontifícia Universidade Católica in the Theories of Culture Lab while carrying out my doctoral research. I worked with the brilliant scholar, Sonia Maria Giacomini, to whom I owe a real debt of gratitude for her wisdom and generosity. I was also briefly affiliated with the NGO Promundo and remain hugely grateful to them for introducing me to the matchless Alice Taylor and Marina Motta, both of whom combine research and practice in inspiring ways. We had a community of friends in Rio who shaped some of my earliest ideas about the city and supported me as a new mother and friend: thank you, Tiffany Kearney, Helen Moestue, Natalie Hoover El Rashidy, and Rachel Fox for your spare bedrooms, your advice, and your love of the city.

As an undergraduate student at the University of Guelph, I was first mentored by Candace Johnson, a gifted feminist thinker and scholar of Latin America. It is not hyperbole to say that I wanted to be just like her when I grew up. At McGill, where this project first started to find its form, my PhD cohort supported and encouraged me in many ways. I am always grateful that my time in Montreal overlapped with Giulia El Dardiry. Her ideas, sharp questions, and insightful comments shaped my work at a very early stage and still do today. My work was molded at McGill by the generous teaching of Eduardo Kohn, Allan Young, Setrag Manoukian, and Tobias Rees. Lisa Stevenson served on my committee and has vastly shaped my anthropological practice. She pushed me to ask questions differently and encouraged me to develop my ethnographic eye, ear, and nose. She is an inimitable example of how to be an anthropologist. Sandra Hyde, my supervisor, was an excellent mentor and now dear friend. She taught me to be, in her words, an "ethnographer's ethnographer." She saw the value of extended time, and life itself, in the field and encouraged me— in her writing and advice—to approach fieldwork and writing as a kind of self making. At McGill, beyond the Anthropology Department, I had the pleasure of being a part of the intellectual and research community in the Department of Whole Person Care. Thank you to Dawn Allen, Tom Hutchinson, and Valerie Badro for your friendship there.

Earlier at MIT I was surrounded by a group of scholars who changed the course of my thinking irrevocably. Thank you to Mia White, Shomon Shamsuddin, Firuzeh Shokooh Valle, all my fellow SPURS fellows, and of course Diane Davis and Bish Sanyal. I am thankful for the mentorship of my supervisor at MIT, Erica Caple James. Her belief in my projects and my ability as a scholar has buoyed me more than once. When I struggled with returning to work after my second maternity leave, Erica ensured that it happened—she engaged with the work, asked tough questions, and then set up spaces where my work could grow and be heard.

At the University of Cambridge I was overwhelmingly welcomed by a group of inspiring anthropologists. Thank you to Chloe Nahum-Claudel, Fiona Wright, Alanna Cant, Sertaç Sehlikoglu, Andrea Grant, Patrick O'Hare, Patrick McKearney, Sian Lazar, Andrew Sanchez, and Rupert Stasch for being unwavering supporters. At Cambridge the Centre of Latin American Studies was a first home. Thank you to Joanna Page, Sarah Radcliffe, and Julie Coimbra for being so open to my work. The CLAS graduate students in the 2016–17 Power and Protest seminar series read my manuscript and gave me some of the most helpful feedback at that stage in my writing: thank you, Catriona Spaven-Donn, Lena Shubman, Ruby Zajac, and Hettie O'Brien. In my other intellectual home at Cambridge, the Centre of Governance and Human Rights, many thanks are owed to Sharath Srinivasan for the opportunities he gave me to grow my work in novel ways.

At the London School of Hygiene and Tropical Medicine, I was part of a community of thinkers that changed my understanding of ethnographic practice and possibility. Thank you Clare Chandler, Susan Nayiga, Christine Nabirye, Miriam Kayendeke, Sarah Staedke, Coll de Lima Hutchison, Justin Dixon, Melissa Parker, Salome Manyau, Komatra Chuengsatiansup, Luechai Sringernyuang, Sittichoke Chawraingern, Thitima Urapeepathanapong, Uravadee Chanchamsang, Wirun Limsawart, Maddy Pearson, and Yuzana Khine Zaw.

I am grateful to Lys Alcayna-Stevens, without whom I would never have finished writing at all. Along with Lys, it was Matt Somerville; Hugh, the cat; and the University of Cambridge Writing Group who taught me how to be a disciplined and joyful writer. Later the Anthro Co-Write Community would be pivotal to me getting this book done.

My thinking on this project, and anthropological sensibilities most broadly, has been shaped by ongoing conversations with a wide range of scholars, who have all taken time to think through ideas and approaches with me. The Atelier community of writers has been unsurpassed in thinking about the creative potential of ethnographic writing. Thank you to Namita Vijay Dharia, Marina Andrea Welker, Lauren Coyle Rosen, Sarah Besky, Duana Fullwiley, Anthony Fontes, Kathryn Mariner, Nomi Stone, Emrah Yildiz, Alessandro Angelini, and Tracie Canada. Thank you especially to Kevin O'Neill for making the Atelier community what it is. Your support on this project has been exceedingly generous. You have been an untiring mentor. This manuscript benefited from an early book workshop, where the most generous group of scholars offered unmatched feedback and advice on my writing. Their shaping of this book cannot be understated: thank you to AbdouMaliq Simone, Jaime Alves, Katie Stewart, Matthew Engelke, Maria José de Abreu, and Susan Lepselter. Thank you too to all who contributed to this book and my thinking in multiple ways, including Kathleen Millar, David Howes, Donna Goldstein, Cymene Howe, Miriam Ticktin, Peter Redfield, David Napier, Jessica Cooper, John Harries, Michael Hathaway, Luísa Reis Castro, Nicolas Fortané, Anne Kelly, Luisa Maria Rivera, Liz Cooper, Maya Mayblin, Robert Samet, Michael Edwards, Méadhbh McIvor, Rebecca Prentice, Dinah Rajak, Genese Sodikoff, Anna Strhan, James Laidlaw, and Chris Garces. Thank you to Chloe Nahum-Claudel and Fiona Wright for key conversations about feminist practice, ethics, and care and all the other life stuff too. You both have been safe harbors. At the University of Edinburgh, a new home, I am grateful to my supportive colleagues and engaged students. At UC Press, many thanks to Kate Marshall. She is a gifted editor, and I count myself extremely lucky to benefit from her support. Much thanks to the entire UC Press team as well, including Susan Silver, my copyeditor, and the design team, who gifted me this beautiful cover. The anonymous reviewers of this book provided clear and critical feedback at a pivotal moment in my thinking. Thank you.

The research would not have been possible without the support provided by the Social Sciences and Humanities Research Council, which awarded me a four-year doctoral fellowship and then augmented it with a further Michael Smith CGS Award to allow for international fieldwork. I am also grateful to the International Development Research Council of Canada, which granted me a Doctoral Research Award (2013–15) and opened the door for my work with Promundo in Rio de Janeiro. McGill also provided generous support in the form of a Provost's Graduate Fellowship (2009), as well as rather extensive support for conference travel. Further financial support in my intellectual growth also came from the Centre of Latin American Studies at the University of Cambridge, the Paul and Priscilla Gray Foundation at the Massachusetts Institute of Technology, and the University of Guelph, which very early on supported and funded both research and Portuguese-language training. Two articles, previously published in *Cultural Anthropology* and *Medical Anthropology: Cross-Cultural Studies in Health and Illness*, have been reworked and are included here. Many thanks to the publishers for the permission to do so.

Finally, I would like to thank my family and dear friends. Thank you to Emma Rooney, who is a continuing example of doggedness and grace. My daughter's fairy godmother, your example is one I want to pass along. Thank you to Shannon Duncan, who came along on our very first visit to Batan—she is always there in my key moments in life, bringing along a kind of matchless magic. These women, along with Sarah Doyle and Gillian Payne, are an enduring sisterhood. They have shaped my feminism, my labor, and my loves. Thank you too to our village family, Lindsey and Tim Russell, and to the women—Ellen, Hannah, and Wendy—who have made Edinburgh a home for us and our children.

My parents are a force of support and good in my life. They gave me freedom, independence, and love like no others. My father was my first intellectual companion: he has shown me what it means to debate, to be curious, and to defy a ticky-tacky future. He is an example of what it means to take a stand but also of how to put in the long, slow, and often unwanted labor of change. My mother is my feminist rock and hard place. I am standing on her shoulders every day, and it is her who my entire core is beholden. My brother, Paul, will always be the companion I was lucky enough to have through some very dark days—he is loyal, stoic, and kind. My family has also always been open to religiosity and the spirit world in all its forms—ghosts come to dinner, the angel of death might join us for an early morning coffee, and fortunes are told with cards. I have been raised in a family that does not bow to convention, and to all of them—especially Mark, Judy, Meryle, Garth, Shirley, Frank, Ruth, Ray, Janice, Lorne, Allison, and Matthew—I owe special thanks. I owe much to Carol and Rod. Beyond the logistics of childcare, they have shown my children and me such a reliable form of love and care. They are an example to live by. My children too deserve thanks. To our daughter, Arden, who has come patiently along through all of this, thank you. She is fire and earth—in other words, a brave and gentle force. Our son, Jude, came along for much of this journey too. His spirit and boundless energy run through all my work. And, finally, thank you to Graham Denyer Willis. You were this book's shepherd—protecting the space, time, and energy needed for me to think and write. Your faith in me and my work is how we got here.

Introduction

ANA'S ANGELS

"You know how the angels piece me and this cart together?" The question comes from Ana, a young Black woman and Evangelical believer living in Rio de Janeiro's *subúrbios*. "My legs and arms become the cart," she continues, "and, as I walk the highway, God holds me and metal together." Ana's typically calm voice is tinged with anxiety as she explains this to me. "The angels piece me and this cart together," she says again, a little firmer now. It's "a way to pray," she insists: this act of patching the cart together—forcing wheels onto axles and carefully slotting the metal sheeting onto each side—is a way to talk with God.

The heavy metal bars hit the pavement with a jarring clank as Ana and the angels work together. The cart is a collection of rusty poles, large wheels, and a few pieces of metal sheeting that need to be assembled again and again each morning, as Ana fears the cart will be stolen if she leaves it intact overnight on her front stoop. She needs it each day for her work delivering bottles of homemade disinfectant to Evangelical shops. So early every morning Ana slides cold metal between hands, gently fitting pieces back together. Using her body as an anchor, she heaves each heavy piece off the cement ledge that borders her home, then twists the parts into place to fit warped metal back together.

1

I can hear her sigh as the cart comes together. Ana exhales in relief. I see her shoulders relax; her tense muscles go slack. Her body folds in toward itself, resting. The cart is still here. No part is too rusty. The wheels still roll. Ana tells me that, amid all the morning noise, no one notices as the angels come to her. The angels sing in her ears as they set to work, she says, and she smiles as they turn her body to steel, piecing skin and metal together. Her limbs now metal, she explains that she is full of God's strength for the day. She tells me, "They turn my body into a *bênção* [blessing]."

She breathes in and pushes her slight body forcefully against the cart. Her bare shoulder—twisted, ready to lever—makes the cart roll forward off the ledge. It holds. Her vessel is worthy. To this feat she responds, "Amen." Ana endures the angel's work with notable cheer. The cart is necessary. So she gives her body over to it. This is God working in her life, she insists. But this work is also painful, and Ana is sometimes uncertain. There have been accidents on the side of the highway. Her arms and legs are scarred, and she has sores that refuse to heal, despite her cheer. The car had swerved, her body and her cart tossed to the side. "No one means to harm me," she says. And yet. "The angels will hold us as we travel today. They won't let us come to harm. The angels hold us tight. They walk this road with us."

THE EXHAUSTED ROUTES OF THE STATE

This book approaches Evangelical faith in Rio's *subúrbios* by attending closely to the choreography of feeling perceptible in Ana's daily work: mercy, joy, and love; duty, pain, and failure. In doing so it demonstrates the centrality of religious desire and sensation to contemporary politics and political subjectivity. Evangelicalism has changed the way people understand the role of the state in their lives as well as citizenship and belonging in Brazil more broadly. It has reoriented political hopes and horizons, such that organized leftist causes and other well-worn routes out of systemic injustice are often cast aside, seen as no longer workable. Evangelicals routinely showed and told me these routes—political recognition, NGO activism, party politics, protests in the street—are exhausted.

The state is not a project they can invest hope in. Instead, they have turned elsewhere. They go with God.

Believers, like Ana, have put their faith in angels. They go with God, not politicians, NGOs, or workers. This kind of belief—and how it transforms both believers and the city itself—is often hard to put into words. Their faith, Evangelicals say, is something they know and sense in their bodies. It is a feeling in the body and shared between bodies: a trace, a pulse, a coursing.[1] Evangelicalism makes people feel worthy, desired, and secure, if only fleetingly. There is a feeling that the angels are there with them, deeming them worthy. People seek this out, which makes sense, as their lives in Rio's *subúrbios* are anything but worthy and secure.

Ana lives in Batan, where I came to live with my partner and children as a PhD student. It is a small favela, a mostly typical community in Rio's suburban landscape.[2] Since the early 1990s Evangelicalism in Rio's western *subúrbios* has become increasingly important, just as it has city- and countrywide. As the Catholic faith slowly dwindles among Brazilians, Evangelical belief surges (Vital da Cunha 2018).[3] The everyday effects of this belief are obvious in the *subúrbios* themselves: makeshift Evangelical churches emerge everywhere, a material testament to the decentralized practices of this way of believing. New Evangelical churches seem to bloom in the cracks; they grow out of corner shops, in store fronts, and even on the steps of people's homes.

Rio is often called the Marvelous City, drawing eyes to the spectacle of particular people, spaces, and topographies. Conjure Rio in your mind's eye. What can you see? The curve of the sea? Jesus on the cliff? The emerald mountains? This iconic city has been so thoroughly lodged in global imaginations—from the city authorities who advertised Rio as an attractive colonial outpost (the "Paris of the tropics") to the foreign pastor returning home to their congregation with tales of their mission work or the traveler with a thin but tantalizing story of being mugged on the beach. In films and photography the idea of Rio has long been crafted along these predictable lines and scales. Its topography, both physical and social, has long provoked attention, with its vibrant favelas nestled into cliffsides, almost but not quite tipping into the affluent leafy streets below. Meanwhile, Ana and the angels piece her cart together on the edge of that spectacle, indeed outside of it. While the term *suburban* often conjures bucolic images of gated communities, Rio's western *subúrbios* tend to be defined from afar as wastelands that bleed out from the marvelous center. Batan sits along Avenida Brasil, a major highway built in the 1940s that bisects the expansive western *subúrbios* it helped expand—a stretch of land about twenty-five miles from Rio's downtown and southside beaches with their neatly tiled promenades. These largely flat and happenstance suburbs are mostly ignored in imaginaries of Rio.

Unlike the favelas that tower over Copacabana and Ipanema's beaches, Rio's *subúrbios* are spaces produced through relegation and commonly imagined as such. They sprawl out from the center; *sprawl* here seems to suggest a kind of overflow or spill, as if urban peripheries are always unplanned and messy, forever informal and grotesque, like a creeping stain on the urban landscape. Like a wasteland, they are imagined as undesirable but also useful as a space where "waste" can be hidden away: prisons, polluting industrial production, public housing, and cheap *diaristas* (day laborers) all find a home here. They exist amid patchwork water pipes and pavement that turns to dirt roads, where cars give way to horse-drawn carts. These suburbs are also always incomplete and provisional; they are new insofar as they repurpose the old from elsewhere.

The banal racialization of the *subúrbios*—the space itself and the people inhabiting this space—is closely connected to the way it is imagined as being peripheral to Rio itself.[4] In public discussion and practice, the *subúrbios* figure in notions of waste—wasteland, human waste, a waste of space. The term *periphery* represents more than just a deficiency of infrastructure and services; it is also used to refer to the Black people who live in them. The racialization of the *subúrbios*—based on a racial hierarchy that privileges whiteness—is in this sense both symbolic and material. Making sense of such encompassing conditions means paying attention to how Black communities were and are systematically disenfranchised, producing a conception of the *subúrbios* as a repugnant periphery. I use the term *subúrbios* throughout this book as a way out of the center/periphery dualism, if imperfectly. I avoid the term *periphery* as a descriptor of place, as I think it reifies the west side's relationship to Rio's center in a way that is not helpful. Using the term *subúrbios* helps in foregrounding the historical processes that construct this enduring dualism, as well as reflecting more local ways of understanding space.[5]

Batan is a community long impacted by the violent oscillations of the state. Three years before I came to Batan, in September 2007, a militia made up of armed off-duty police agents ousted the Amigos dos Amigos, a prison-based organization that had held and governed the community for more than two decades. In the western *subúrbios*, as elsewhere in this city, the everyday governance of communities has long been fractured and over-lapping, divided between organizations born out of mass incarceration and *milícias* (parapolice groups organized and made up of off-duty police offic-ers and firefighters). Numerous *milícias* originated out of a local desire to "reclaim" their communities from gangs. Many, however, became blatant rent extractors and rudimentary protection rackets, with shady connec-tions to electoral politics, "taxing" the informal economy and the people who live in the communities they govern on everything from internet access and van transportation to operating a motorcycle taxi and running businesses—and, of course, for security itself. They also govern under the threat of extreme violence, much like the drug traffickers before them.

Less than a year after the militia took over, several journalists from the well-known Brazilian newspaper *O Dia* moved into Batan to conduct an undercover investigative report on the rise of Rio's militias, which had garnered increased attention for their use of violence and shadow-state activities. The journalists wanted to get a good story about these parastate operatives, their links to the illicit economies of the favelas, and their vio-lence. Less than two weeks after their arrival in Batan, however, the jour-nalists' cover was blown. On the night of May 16, 2008, six militia mem-bers forced their way into the journalists' rented house, demanding all of their video and audio recordings. When the search was unsuccessful, the militia members became violent. They held a journalist, photographer, and driver hostage and tortured them for over six hours. After electrocut-ing them, they began asphyxiating them with plastic bags, while threaten-ing to drop them off in a neighboring public-housing block where they believed traffickers would discover and kill them (Claudino 2011).

This case placed a spotlight on the prevalence and violence of militias in the city more broadly. Whereas the municipal and national governments of Rio and Brazil had previously been outwardly ambivalent about militias, this violence against recognized public figures generated public pressure to respond. Rio's state government established a Parliamentary Inquiry with a remit to investigate militia prevalence across the city, including the links between militias and local and municipal politicians (Assembléia Legislativa 2008). In 2009, one year before I moved to Batan with my family, to appear to decisively resolve this episode between the militia and journalists, Rio's special operations policing unit—Batalhão de Operações Policiais Especiais—"pacified" Batan, taking the favela back and creating the possibility for state governance. Batan, a small and remote community in Rio's West Zone, had gone from a site of age-old historical neglect to a witness of the state's vision of who must be protected and why.

Almost everyone I know in Batan has been harmed through this and other forms of racialized violent policing.[6] When pacification forces arrived, people remained ambivalent or aloof, almost as though it didn't really matter who the men with guns were: no matter who they were, they still did the same things—confronted you, accosted you, got in your way, or did the same to someone you knew. For most the pacification force was understood through logics of state violence and imposition, another extension of how both historical and present conditions of harm defined their everyday lives, from poverty to injury to precarious work to lack of infrastructure like clean water, safe roads, and hospitals and clinics. These discussions of violence were always also discussions of racism. Denise Ferreira da Silva describes these "pacification" campaigns as military occupations, made possible through "kill on the spot" policing, military-grade helicopters shooting into the streets with automatic weapons, and armed vehicles patrolling streets, as happened in Batan. Da Silva argues that this "formulation of racial violence . . . captures the way in which raciality immediately justifies the state's decision to kill some people . . . in the name of self-preservation. These exterminations do not trigger an ethical crisis because the bodies of these people and the territories they inhabit almost always already signify violence" (2014, 69). As Jaime Alves (2014) puts it, writing on the way Black life is governed and rendered destructible, life in Brazil for Black people is imbued with an "ordinary" "anti-black terror," in which Blackness is read as a sickness of the individual and of space and named as disorder, authorizing the killing of Black life.[7] Or as Christen A. Smith extends this self-preservation of the state through anti-Black violence: "The black body in pain" is part of the organization of Brazil. "Brazil's horizon of death erases the black body. . . . This is not to say that blackness can truly be reduced to this state of death and invisibility, but rather that this is the political project of state terror" (2016, 175).

These suburbs, pacified or not, are entrenched with everyday reminders of terror's proximity to themselves, their families, and their communities. They are often places of acute physical and social abandonment, made and enacted through this systemic anti-Blackness. In the height of the dry season, when the water supply is low, the city water company—a public-private partnership—shuts the taps here so others at the beach front can enjoy access without disruption. In other seasons floods caused by inadequate wastewater infrastructure regularly fill people's homes with knee-high water. Infants die of preventable causes in crowded hospitals that offer only marginal prenatal care. This is a city, and a form of governance, premised on the disposability, capture, and dispossession of Black life (Vargas 2018).

Evangelicalism in Batan, and the *suburbios* more broadly, cannot be separated from these violent whims of the state. We must situate Evangelicalism within this ongoing violence and consider how Evangelical belief and practice are ways of making sanctuary: spaces of respite from the ordinary operations of state abandonment and capture.[8] The Evangelicalism that I describe in this book is widely believed to be knotted together with the rule of the former Far Right president of Brazil, Jair Bolsonaro, whose presidency was buoyed by Evangelicals across Brazil. Yet the kinds of violent exclusion and harm that Bolsonaro lauded and incentivized, his efforts to borrow from Evangelicalism and its currents, both preceded him and will outlast him. His presidency should be seen as both violent and neofascist in organization. At the same time, his loss in the 2022 election should not be mistaken for the departure of cruelty.

This book grapples with the ways that popular Evangelicalism transcends electoral politics, linked to many Evangelicals' exhaustion and mistrust with both the political Left and Right. This mistrust can resettle into hope, in part because Evangelicalism has come to offer up something of a departure from the misgivings that have long surrounded political rhetoric and inconsistent political action, even in the face of sprawling need. It can't be denied that bombastic Evangelicals do tremendous harm through multiple forms of violence, including the persecution of LGBTQ individuals and communities, systemic racism, gender-based violence, and the ongoing wage theft from people when they are at their most miserable and vulnerable. Bolsonaro capitalized on all of this, packaging his message in high-profile Evangelical pastors' promises, offering up a state project seemingly in God's grace and favor. The violence that came with his presidency (and after) is deplorable; as has been the violence of absent care, police massacres, and racial subordination through Brazil's history. I encourage readers to critically engage with this book's depiction of Evangelicalism as something that certainly emerges from violence and harm and also from individuals' and families' desperation for safety: a modicum of grace in the city.

·   ·   ·   ·   ·

Clank.
Clank.
Clank.
Clank.

It's Ana again, putting together her cart. She tells me that she graciously holds out her arms to the angels and then sits neatly on the stoop so that they might more easily turn her limbs to metal, converting her body into a prayer, a blessing, a vessel.

The sounds rouse me each morning. The sharp metallic scraping and dinging of heavy metal bars being dragged, dropped, and forced together wakes everyone on this strip of the street: a 4:45 a.m. call to prayer. Soon the clanking is joined by the sounds of dogs, shuffling feet, televisions, and maybe the hum of the water pump—that is, if someone has neglected to fill the rooftop tank the evening before. A military plane suddenly rumbles a few hundred feet overhead. The morning smells begin to waft over too: sweet coffee, soapy laundry water, petrol fumes. These smells simmer on the hot pavement in the summer or in the dampness that clings to air, nostrils, and asbestos roof tiles in the rainy months.

Ana and her extended family—three adults and six children—live together on the ground floor of a self-built home. They have lived in Batan for many years. They all migrated from the port city of São Luís in the state of Maranhão, a comparatively tiny city, located in the far northeastern tip of the country. Many migrants to the western *subúrbios* come from there, moving down south in the early phases of Brazilian urbanization, with some later migrants following their Evangelical networks. Ana first migrated to live with her Evangelical brother and his family, but she has since also heard God's call through the angels. Now she too is a *crente* (believer). Eighteen-year-old Ana moved to Batan when she was not quite sixteen. She has a two-year old daughter, Hannah, whom she is raising on her own. She laughs out loud—an uncommon occurrence for her—when I ask if she'd like to move back to São Luís. She says, "There isn't enough food for the chickens in São Luís, Laurie, and there is no São Luís to go back to anyways."

This morning I join Ana in the street. We set off together after loading the cart with her aunt's homemade disinfectant, which she bottles in repurposed plastic soda bottles and sells widely. We push the cart down the street toward the highway on our way to the first shop, where we will distribute half of the bottles. We travel through Batan, away from the main square. We go the longer way around to avoid the highway side for as long as we can. I find the cart trickier to push than I had imagined: the wheels don't ever quite go where you want them to go. It is pieced together with bits and scraps found in Batan. Nothing is wasted—there is a bicycle wheel on one side and a wheel from a different bike on the other. The bars are repurposed from nearby construction projects, and the tarpaulin cover, gifted by a neighbor, is secured with a refashioned pole previously used to build scaffolding. I hesitate as we approach the sandy shoulder of highway. My son is with me in his baby carrier, and he's still squirming. He hasn't fallen asleep like I'd hoped, and I'm already hot and tired with the sharpening sun landing on my shoulders. We've barely begun. It would be easy to stop here and wish her well. Ana senses my hesitation and slows slightly. But I push on to keep pace, readjusting the carrier straps, and we keep moving.

We move down the large highway that links the suburbs to the center, passing the industries that have, historically and today, been magnets for people looking to settle, find jobs, and survive. The highway runs through national military lands, where new recruits are trained. It is also the site where the 2016 Olympic shooting range (the Centro Olímpico de Tiro) was constructed. Jets and army cargo planes fly practice tours over Batan. The military-adjacent lands are lush and well tended; there is a large farm where goats graze. These lands are carefully closed off at all potential entry points, with near ten-foot razor-wire fences blocking the way. There is a firefighter training camp here too. The training base often runs emergency scenarios, setting fire to buildings, trucks, and debris just to the side of the highway. The ensuing smoke clouds the roads, billowing into the open doors of *kombis* (the twelve-seater vans that operate informally to rush people through the city). In the heat of the day, the dark smoke barely dissipates. Instead, it hovers over the public-housing blocks, the makeshift housing along the commuter train line, churches, and shopping malls.

We eventually arrive at a large pedestrian overpass that links one neighborhood to another across the highway. The overpass is a hovering cement structure with blue side rails. We walk up one side on a steep ramp and then switchback to a less steep but longer path that leads up to the bridge. Limbs shaking, we cross over with the cart. On the downside we both hang on and pull back hard on the cart so it doesn't rush out ahead of us. We walk into the neighboring community and head straight for the main square. We turn into a small shop owned by a couple who also attend one of the Evangelical churches that Ana's family attends weekly. They take over half of the bottles of disinfectant from the cart; they'll sell them in their shop, and Ana will collect the money later. After that Ana and I push the cart back out to the street, return over the bridge, and head straight to a nearby public-housing block. Ana delivers the last of the disinfectant bottles two at a time to another shop, also owned by a fellow Evangelical, who runs her shop out of her small apartment. This time I stay outside, standing guard over the cart. Ana moves up and down the maze of concrete steps, bottles in hand, her feet slapping cement. When Ana returns, the cart is empty, and we begin our walk home. Once there, sitting safe on the stoop and drinking cold soda, I ask Ana if the angels walked with us this morning.

"Yes," she tells me, confidently. "Every morning I ask the angels for the grace to continue my work." She clasps my hands in hers, and we are joined on the steps by her sister-in-law, who leads us in a prayer. We've distributed all the disinfectant, and they are already at work making more. As I get ready to leave, they both tell me to *"vai com Deus"* (go with God). It's a common—even banal—parting here, uttered by almost everyone, regardless of faith. But this morning I check the sky when they say it, to see if the angels are there.

GRACEFUL ELABORATIONS

What does it mean for Ana to ask the angels for grace? To desire and seek grace in this city? She moves through the city accompanied by angels who contort her body and simultaneously protect her from harm. The cart she pushes appears to be subject to an unbridgeable impasse. On the one hand, it is a piecemeal metal contraption assembled of and through waste in a risk-laden landscape of precarity. On the other hand, it is a divine gift of grace: her body and cart crafted together by angels into a *bênção* that comes from elsewhere. Ana is open here about her optimism regarding the divine and its cruelties. She doesn't try to hide the work's pain. Instead, Ana puts that pain to work to describe how the desire for grace—and the reasons behind that desire—are both compelling and problematic. She is aware of how her act of prayer bends her body, forcing it into particular arrangements. It asks her to become resilient, where resilience seems to be about encouraging bodies to endure so they will not succumb to pressure—so they can take the pain, "so they can keep taking it; so they can take more of it" (Ahmed 2017, 189).[9]

Grace is profoundly sensory. Evangelicalism opens new sensations of possibility for people to feel emancipated. Evangelicalism has the power to make people feel removed from feelings of abandonment or restriction, describing the sensation of being lifted from all that has so cruelly and cunningly captured them, tied them down, and sought to destroy them. These sensations are often described as saving—graceful—experiences. When you are in it, you feel worthy, lifted above the fray of the visible world. Conversely, when the feeling withers, deflates, or suddenly dissipates, you can feel lost, cold, and untouchable. While the urge to create and feel these sensations are rooted in individual and collective histories of violence and governance by abandonment in the city and beyond, these sensations are strangely atemporal. By doing something as simple as participating in a charismatic prayer circle or piecing together a cart in the company of angels, believers are searching for the *whoosh*. This is a sensation often evoked by sighing deeply while making a *whooshing* noise as one's arms and shoulders relax and one's body tips forward, much like letting down a heavy load. Believers explain that bodily exhalation and lightness as a stretch of time in which they are lifted above the fray—swept away from the historical and present conditions of material and systemic violence that too commonly define them and their spaces. It is through these desires, acts, and doings that they describe their desire to be with God, to go with God, to know and feel that God cares for them and their futures.

Yet those who describe these experiences are also keenly aware of their vulnerability. As for Ana, there is anxiousness about her belief. These sensations tend to waft, harden, dissipate, and return. The feeling of lightness might linger for a moment, an evening, maybe even months, but it is far from permanent. Rather—like a good perfume or even a stench—it is in and out, very much there and then completely gone, untraceable, simply a figment or recollection until—*whoosh*—there it is, back again, an emotional assault.

Whoosh, here is that feeling of being worthy.

Whoosh, here is that feeling of being desperately worthless again.

Evangelicals speak of this sensation as something like *graça* (grace), beauty, an overflowing joy, and a weight being lifted. Grace is a kind of renunciation of the world they have been dealt. As one believer said, grace means being "in God's arms." The sheer lightness of the *whoosh*, to be carried, lifted, recognized, and enjoyed.

This sensory experience of grace is not simply theological. It's also political: an experience through which Evangelicals devise new ways of living together, outside of the gaze of the state. Theologically speaking, grace is the eternal promise of salvation given by God through everlasting love and protection.[10] Among Evangelicals in Batan, grace was both gift and renunciation. Grace, given and received by God and found within their communities, is understood as a form of disavowal, a rejection of a wretched world, and an elaboration of a different kind of life and living. Here I think about Saidiya Hartman's (2017) depiction of the "slum" as an "arena of elaboration," an "urban commons where the poor assemble, improvise the forms of life, experiment with freedom, and refuse the menial existence scripted for them." Thinking of grace as an elaboration means reckoning with it as a theory of belonging and worth. A graceful elaboration is a reconfiguration of space and life, an urgent remaking of the value of lives in a city hell-bent on harm. To ask for grace on the outskirts of this city is to make a radical demand; to give it is a radical gesture. It feels so good. Its absence feels bottomless.

Grace as an elaboration is, as Ashon Crawley (2017) writing on Black Pentecostalism renders for us, a kind of "otherwise possibility" tethered to histories and an ongoing present of anti-Blackness. For Crawley, an otherwise is not new but rather a reminder that "alternative modes, alternative strategies, alternative ways of life *already* exist" (6–7). Grace as an elaboration within a world intent on anti-Blackness is a move toward an "otherwise" that, as Crawley writes, "bespeaks the ongoingness of possibility" (24–25).[11]

In this book I consider how contemporary Evangelical practice in Rio's western *subúrbios* has upended rote boundaries and become a project of imagining the city—and especially the suburbs—in different ways. Evangelical belief inverts assumptions about Rio's largely Black peripheries: it gives new meaning to the peripheral experiences of abandonment, precarity, and insecurity. A graceful elaboration of hope and emancipation is a way for Evangelicals to imagine a different kind of future for themselves and their families. In a city where to be governed often means to be made disposable, Evangelicalism affirms life and upends normative ideas about who belongs and why; it supersedes the so-called citizenship project and the governance of life in the margins.

Given the way Evangelicalism has been used by right-wing politicians in Brazil to bolster their own rise and domination, it is not uncomplicated to think of grace as an otherwise elaboration that affirms Black life in Rio. It would be understandable to take the opposite approach: that Evangelicalism is rather antithetical to an antiracist politics that upholds Black life in this city. My attention to grace here is concerned exactly with this perplexing push and pull of desire and manipulation. Evangelical belief cannot be reduced to people somehow being duped by a series of false promises from politicians or pastors. But it also cannot be separated from coercion, desperation, and a longing for better. While the kind of belief that I outline in this book occurs in a landscape of violence, to write off Evangelical belief as little more than a neoliberal problem child of Brazil or the consequence of right-wing propaganda eclipses how it reorganizes the everyday experiences of social life, assuring a newfound optimism, even while that optimism roots itself in pain, violence, and precarity and is filled with promises that so often go unkept.[12]

Much has been written of Rio's spatial entanglements between the *morro* (hill) and the *asfalto* (pavement) and the formal/informal nexus in urban Brazil more broadly. But such scalar and topographic representations obscure a much larger urban field, especially around the mundane flatlands of the *subúrbios*. I show how the *subúrbios* have their own contemporary and historical, spatial, and political origins and their own histories of urban migration and displacement, labor, ecology, and—more acutely now—religion. This work prioritizes the lived experiences of the *subúrbios*, with attention to their religions, livelihoods, families, security, and governance. Here we might think of the *suúrbios* as elaborations too—not just material extensions of the city but also theories themselves of what a city is, an elaboration on the possible.[13] In turn I focus on how suburban space-making practices feel, are moved through, and are generative. I bring out why it matters that Evangelicalism has captivated the *suúrbios* more so than the center of Rio. In Rio's *suúrbios* religious, political, and space-making practices are graceful elaborations, revealing how people imagine what is good and safe, right and honorable, valued and ethical—in concrete and fences, certainly, but also through shared dreams, visions, and sensations.

The Evangelical promise enables a sense of hope, optimism, and salvation, but this optimism is tethered to a violent conception of the state, its actors and quasi actors, and its histories and present-day landscape of racialized violence, abuse, and pain. A graceful elaboration is an invitation, in which grace—as a theory—is a kind of speculation. It is a speculative feeling, desire, and experimentation in making politics meaningful to real life, such that it is not dependent on a contained and individualized citizen-subject or the idea that politics and political life is only about certain kinds of spaces—like a voting booth or a march on the central plaza. The Evangelicals I lived with articulate and practice a form of care of self and community that is not dependent on the state and indeed supersedes it. For many believers, if their relationship to the state has been defined largely by violence and disavowal, then the spaces they now seek to build are not attempts to correct the state through models of citizenship, inclusion, and reform. Rather, they are concerned with collective and collaborative projects of envisioning and building something new: spaces of grace in the city through God and community. Evangelicalism in suburban Rio has become the means to elaborate on futures beyond: a radical mercy for themselves. Evangelicals attune themselves to a felt experience of grace.[14] They go with God.

.   .   .   .   .

"Do you believe in angels?" Ana asks.

Do I? I ask myself. I was raised in the church. I'm the daughter of a minister. I am no longer religious, but I used to be. I know what it is to be comfortable in church and in its kinds of community and to begin and end each day with prayer. I spent my childhood in the church's stiff pews and scratchy cushions, listening hard to its layers of promises and truths, its landscapes of belief pulling at my body, heart, and spirit. I was a teenager in its vast parking lots, driving to Christian youth groups on Sunday afternoons and their summer camps in hot July weeks. I know what it is for politics to be lived through church in mundane, institutional, and humanitarian ways.

My father, a leftist dreamer-preacher, brought his politics to the pulpit each week. He was a natural storyteller, and I watched how he made people nod along throughout a sermon. By the end of each sermon, they would still be nodding—without doubt. This was his calling: watching people dream with him. It was what made it all worthwhile. His eschatological doctrine (his end-of-days scenario) rested in the idea that life itself was God's dream. The inherent threat in this somewhat benign image is that God could at any moment wake up. Live your life now, he'd imply, because isn't it obvious God has been sleeping a long time?

My mother, raised in the Baptist Church by an Irish Catholic father, is a social worker. She'd been forced to learn to play the piano as a young girl just in case she ever married a minister, which she did when she was seventeen. When I went to Uganda at twenty years old to work for a rights-based NGO, it was my father's parishioners, my mother's social-work colleagues, and my friends from Conrad Grebel, a progressive Mennonite college at the University of Waterloo, who threw my going-away party. If conversion was not our goal, we were nevertheless part of a project that understood development and humanitarianism as a single, discrete mission, a form of being called. When Evangelicals speak to me about their own callings, I remember what it felt like—this sensation that God was knocking at your heart, the sensation of desire that accompanied wanting to be called.

As someone who struggles with depression, I still talk to the angels when I'm falling into shadow. It is a habit bred in pew, blood, and song. Despite no longer being a believer, calling out to Jesus and his angels has been ingrained in me, especially in times of fear and despair. From the shadow, fearful and most vulnerable, the urge to call out to angels rings true in my ears.

EVANGELICAL POSSIBILITIES

Go with God is a tunnel of a book, rooting between spaces and sensations often ephemeral and fluid, both optimistic and harmful. I am intent on paying attention to the sheer amount of work it takes to arrive somewhere else and to feel something different. I am also intent to uncover how a politics is constituted through these endeavors. My account of Evangelicals' attempts to encounter and elaborate on grace attends to the tentative optimism with which they negotiate grace and to how this process unfolds within particular spaces and bodies.[15]

First, I track the sensory life of bodies and the actual materials, scents, and textures with which people touch, smell, move, dwell, and make; I show how religious sensations are cultivated, enforced, and desired. I do this with ethnographic attention to how people move and reside in the *subúrbios,* from the factories where they work to the transportation, water, and health systems they use, and consider how they then mold their faith lives around these practices and itineraries. I look at how people use their bodies to pray, to seek, and to feel God and how doing so reorganizes communities: how it compels the renovation and reconstruction of houses and sidewalks into sanctuaries, how it alters the ways the city is moved through and experienced via divine shopping carts and drink trollies, and how it nurtures the hunt for both angels and demons. Through this I show how grace is material, felt, and sought in people's everyday lives and how the materiality of grace comes to matter for the sustenance and constitution of salvific life in the city.

Crawley writes that the sensual practices of Black religious practice is critical for conceptualizing its radical political stakes and potential: "performative dances, songs, noises, and tongues illustrate how enjoyment, desire, and joy . . . [speak] back against aversion, embarrassment, and abandonment, against the debasement and denigration of blackness" (2017, 6–7). Attending to the very material and sensual life of Evangelicalism, in ways both lively and joyful and equally under pressure and duress, resists a flat representation of the politics of religion, community, and city. Turning to the sensory experience of religion foregrounds the body as a scene of celebration *and* governance but also unveils the radical potential of bodily experience as a cradle for political elaboration: what gets felt in the body is itself a way to make and build theory in the city and beyond. The *whoosh* and its retreat are experiences that can be elaborated into ways of thinking about the world differently.

At the second, theoretical level, this book asks what we can learn if we think about grace as politics itself. I ask this purposefully, not as a way to sidestep concerns about the alignment between Evangelicalism and right-wing electoral politics in Brazil but to engage both differently. So much of this book is about exhaustion, both political and bodily. For Evangelicals in Rio's suburbs, the state manifests most frequently as a series of seemingly endless promises of the state yet to come and as a set of modes of citizenship and rights that have long been promised but never materialized—except, perhaps, as forms of capture. The state is understood as pinning people down, eating them up, exhausting and destroying them. People were always tired, they said, because their work was like Ana's: piecemeal, precarious, and often dangerous, with long and unpredictable hours and no job security or benefits and with the state as a specter of regulation and violent intervention rather than care. Ana knew this. She explained how her body is often in pain, and she is constantly tired. She is tired out by this labor, the early mornings, the demands of raising a young child on her own, and never knowing if there will be enough to get by each month.

For others it is a constant hustle to find a job, maneuvering through limited and unpredictable transit, fixing a broken car or motorcycle without the money to do so, waiting a half day in the clinic and still not being seen by a doctor, enduring the electric company cutting power to coerce people into signing an energy contract, or encountering horse manure in the playground. This is layered with visceral fear: a police state of normalized terror against Black communities and individuals, producing a ubiquitous buzz of anxiety in the streets. Anxiety is like a ringing in the ear. The state—both current and promised—is too commonly deemed a fool's route for correcting any of this. Evangelicalism—and its promise of grace—is often embodied and evoked as a joyful and restful route out of exhaustion's loops and summons: moments, expanses, and spaces of rejuvenation such as a prayer circle, an angel next to you by the highway, a healing ceremony, a preacher who can hear a personal message from God to you. In a place where people are continually burdened, God's grace is respite. There is something to be found in refusal—in refusing the state's advances where possible, in refusing to see themselves as the state seems to see them, as either criminals or victims, either lost to or belonging to the wastelands of the *subúrbios* and the favelas. There is something significant to instead claim the *subúrbios* as God's place, their place.

This book understands grace as a mode of making politics beyond the state. In this sense grace counters the violence embedded in the continuous assumption that "the state is both inevitable and recuperable" (Shange 2019, 3). A politics of state recuperation treats the state like a convalescent loved one, something that must be revived at all costs, even while acknowledging the innumerable harms done both directly and through disavowal and dispossession. I dwell in the ways that grace is a form of political hope too, a recuperation of space and self and community, but maybe less recognizably so. It relieves a burden. Grace might be best understood as a way to rejuvenate under a set of violent political conditions. It might be less durable or legible than, say, a protest or an election, but it is still a way to pursue a future less tied to the assumption of durability in the first place: to go with the politics of God, not with the politics of the state.

Finally, this book is also about the aesthetics and possibilities of ethnographic representation. This is a sensory-immersive book, focused on the complex play between textual representation, ethnographic form, and argument. I ask the reader to reside with the presence of angels. Throughout my fieldwork, often consumed by insecurity, abandonment, and heartbreak—and regularly in profound misery—Ana asked me to train my eyes, ears, nose, and touch on the presence of angels.[16] Writing this book has become an experiment in representing these registers in ethnographic texture on the page. How does one gracefully render an angel? To do so I opted for a sensory-attuned ethnographic practice, through and with the sensory life of bodies and how they move through particular spaces. As I have tried to practice it, a sensory ethnography of these suburbs involves an attention to the relation between the senses and the otherwise. Sensory ethnography opens up possibilities for tending to the ephemeral, the unsure, the incoherent, the attempt, the fleeting, and the incomplete. This attention is to all the ways that bodily feeling is important for understanding how people make sense of their worlds and futures. If the subject of this book is Evangelicalism and the suburbs, it is equally about the methods of holding on to that which is often ephemeral, crushed, or trampled, only ever a *whoosh*. This book therefore slows down. It experiments with a mode of representation that resists the narrative urge to push forward and instead dwells in body and feeling. This involves paying attention to the tensing of muscle and tendon, the stretch of an arm, a stomachache, the extension of a vowel in the word *hello*. It involves paying attention to how spatiality gets intuited, generated, even stomached.

A central commitment of this book—told just as much in form as in argument—is that pace and punctuation matter for an ethnography of sensory life and bodies, in terms of how we remain open to the multiplicity of possibilities embedded in any transitory moment. This book draws attention to the body as it weaves between wafting sensorial accounts, mundane aches, decentered struggle, and the more typically asphalt-like presents and material landscapes where this sensing occurs. Certain forms of text and interview seem to constitute captivity, but telling stories differently can offer fracture lines, unexpected openings and departures. As Lisa Stevenson writes, the "imagistic rather than discursive modes of knowing" are a kind of uncertain hatch—if we open them, they require us to listen and engage differently (2014, 10). Tuning into the body—to smell, movement, touch, sound, making, and texture, through both textual practice and visual form—can recalibrate the frequency and scale of a story and the work it does and what it is being asked to do. In turn the body is always present in the writing. I consider how bodies move through space, where bodies are sniffing, glaring, and eavesdropping, working not as contained subjects but as feeling bodies that must move and attach themselves in landscapes where power surges and amuses. Ethnographic description—in its multiplicities of forms—can dig tunnels between the space of the body and the worlds that bodies move in. This kind of description is a careful practice of thinking through angles, lines and drips, lays and overlays—a palimpsest of all the ways bodies are cared for, harmed, desired, and rebuked.

TUNNELING THROUGH A MANUSCRIPT

As a guest in Batan, I was forever glimpsing the *subúrbios* and its Evangelical fervor from unanticipated vantage points: a shared memory of a childhood bedroom window, a dusty boulder, a lovers' motel now abandoned, or on my knees in prayer. Later on I saw them through WhatsApp messages sent from hospitals without oxygen, homespun Evangelical podcasts, and Live on Facebook church services. Ethnography is often the practice of being invited into these unanticipated vantage points that leave you changed because you hadn't anticipated that a world could unfurl in a moment, sweeping you away from customary forms of knowing, seeing, and sensing. The work of turning it all into the something that you hold in your hands is a strange and anxious project: turning the fleetingness of Evangelical fervor into something so permanent, to be somehow contained in a sentence, an image, or an argument. A lot is at stake in these moves, especially given the ongoing violence that Evangelicalism has come to traffic in and uphold within Brazil today and historically. I am anxious about remaining open to ways that people desire to be saved and what they understand they are being saved from. I am anxious about what these descriptions of Evangelical belief evade and are being asked to do. I am anxious about what it means to believe in angels and demons and wolves in the city: their delicate touch and their violent intrusions.

As such, the book is less an expansive opening than a tunnel, on purpose: tunnels can take us to new spaces but also leave us uncertain about where we are and how we arrived there and the terrain we bypassed to reach a destination. A tunnel is a way into something, a passageway, a designed and dug-out route, a labor meant to transport you somewhere else. But tunnels are also binding. The result of this work is a book characterized by abstraction, assemblage, and fragmentary glimpses. Indeed, ethnographic writing is a bit like tunneling: an intervention on the land, disruptive and disorienting. With hope you arrive somewhere else by the end. The chapters each tunnel in distinctive ways.

Chapter 1 considers what I call a politics of avowal through an attention to violence, loss, grief, and the forms of community and togetherness that emerge from a loss of hope in political systems. I tell this story through the death of a newborn child in a local and vastly underfunded suburban hospital. I use that term *avowal* to contemplate the hard edge of grace: the space of wreckage from which a desire for grace emerges, what almost breaks you, taking you to your knees.

Chapter 2 turns to the things that have the potential to uplift: the pieces of grace in the margins that have the capacity to both transform and mediate the relationship among Evangelicals and the divine and even the city itself. I consider the very materiality of grace through the way these scraps become religious goods to be touched, molded, put together, and remade and how religious sensoriums are constituted through religious mediation. Here I think about the ways that the city itself is given new form—through roadside churches, for example, or pieced-together carts that roll through the city, crossing boundaries typically uncrossable. "Following the thing" (Cook 2004), then, also became about following the grace of the thing, something akin to an optimistic attachment (Berlant 2011) and possibility located in a thing, scrap, or fragment. At the same time, I pay attention to the limits—to the unbearable weight of optimism on a life.

Chapter 3 is ostensibly an accounting of the military-led pacification campaign enacted in the local community where this research took place just prior to my arrival. This was a military operation meant to oust a militia made up of off-duty police and firefighters. I tell the story of pacification through the story of a wound that won't heal and the attempts at healing that are made and sought, within health systems and within the Evangelical community. What I track in this chapter is the shifting presence and absence of the state and the forms of ongoing violence embedded in a notion of abandonment. I think of abandonment as a kind of unmitigated uncertainty or the mundane intent to harm, building from a collection of works that critically considers how Brazil's cities are made, contorted, and put to use constituting unequal outcomes for those who call these cities their home (Caldeira 2000; Donna Goldstein 2003; Holston 2008; Robb Larkins 2015). I consider what forms of grace endure or are newly made here and what a graceful kind of future making looks like in everyday life through an attention to wounds—how they get made and how they heal (or don't).

Chapter 4 moves back and forth through different moments and arrangements of crises in the city of Rio in the 2010s. I think about the ways that racism obliterates neat notions of citizenship, advancing conversations about engagement and expectations of the state and in turn the forms of conservatism that have been popular among Evangelicals. Here I attend to the significant political shifts seen in Brazil over the past decade, culminating in the election of a Far Right president, Jair Bolsonaro. Today the *subúrbios* are often defined by outsiders by their militia governance and their burgeoning Evangelicalism. To liberals from the center, suburban believers are characterized as the dupes of right-wing political machinery, suffering under a false consciousness and not knowing what is good for them—that is, human rights, welfare, and sensible and orderly systems of state governance and justice. To those on the Right, believers are also approached as a kind of dupe: lost souls to be hunted and claimed, enlisted in the army of heaven that enriches certain elites' pockets here on earth, while the foot soldiers of God are left to wait for the riches of the kingdom. I attempt to move beyond these binary coordinates, continuing to unfold a story of how Evangelical faith in the *suúrbios* reorganizes the very meaning of the city and its crises, along with the political imaginations and aspirations of grace it might mold, contain, and unravel and the kinds of electoral politics it embraces and refuses along the way.

Chapter 5 considers the work of demons, both symbolic and real, and the ways they haunt the landscape of the *suúrbios*. I turn to stories of drug addiction, gang affiliations, gender-based violence, and precarity to show how Evangelicals think about demons as constantly nipping at their heels, hiding in the shadows, and preying on them in the streets. I show how demons are used to understand feelings of gracelessness, moments of betrayal, deception, and collapse. When you can't find grace, the demons can find you. Failure is not a foreclosure or the kind of structure that bedevils the future but a possibility. Failure is a story about what once was and may still be a potential. In the conclusion I bring these strands together to think through what an attention to Evangelicals' religious feeling reveals about cities, space, and power in Brazil today. I do so to contemplate what a politics of grace in Rio might entail and reckon with this in relation to the harm and manipulation done by Evangelical politicians.

1 Avowal

On the edge of the city, on the edge of the hillside, Jovina and I stand with our arms lifted above our heads. We push out our chests and raise our eyes to the sky. We stand in the shadow of a colossal boulder—an aberration of the landscape—that marks one's arrival to Batan. It balances seemingly perilously on the edge of the grassy hilltop. To one side of us are miles of Brazilian military land and training stations, where mostly young and poor men complete their mandatory military terms—that is, men who lack a university spot that might have excused them. On the other side we look out over the main highway that moves people and goods in and out of Rio's famous *centro* (downtown). A large mountain range hovers in the distance, dividing this patch of land from all that supposedly matters in this iconic city. An arid wind hangs in the valley; even on the hillside there is little reprieve from the persistent dry heat that hardens rock, crumbles dirt, and yellows grass.

The boulder is a marker. It's a physical marker, a landmark, but also a spiritual marker—even a guarantor—of God's divine presence here. If Rio de Janeiro's center has a manmade Jesus to watch over it, the west has this instead: an enduring and imposing reminder to people that they have built their house on the rock, not faulty sands. I am here with Jovina, an

Evangelical believer. She prays loudly, hands in the air, fingers wiggling at Jesus. Her long fingers dance in the air as she prays like she's reaching for piano keys in the sky, but the music of her voice crumbles down the rock like an avalanche. Full of grief, there is no wind for her voice to float on. It feels like Jesus can't be reached today. As the prayers dwindle down, I turn and ask Jovina if this is a "thin" place. She's never heard the expression, so I elaborate, "Is this a place where heaven and earth meet?" Jovina shakes her head in further discouragement, like I've misunderstood something simple. She says, "You don't need thin places to feel heaven. Batan is a place of God." On the edge of this city, on the edge of this hillside, "God resides here," she intones heavily.

After praying, Jovina and I linger on the hillside a little longer. The hike up the hill requires moving through long grass on a rocky but well-trampled path, cut by the thousands of feet moved to visit the stone and pray each year. We've come before the heat has broken, just before dusk, to have it to ourselves. In the early evening many will come to the hillside with a pastor for a small service, and on Friday and Sunday evenings many more will gather here. But for now it is just us, and we hide in the bits of shade cast by the boulder, standing close together. I've been here many times, but this is my first time with Jovina. She is eager to share it with me. I kick at the hot dust and sit down, but Jovina remains standing. I've known Jovina since I moved here, as she and her family were among the first people we met in Batan. She's a Black woman in her fifties and has been a *crente* (believer) for almost three decades.

We continue to linger, looking out over this part of the city together. We are reluctant to move on, both lost in our own thoughts. Our prayers today are for Jovina's daughter, who just a week ago lost her newborn baby only hours after her birth. Her name was Megan. Jovina's body is heavy as we move down the hillside. There was no grace to be found there this evening. No lightness on the breeze of prayer to catch and uplift. A grandchild of hers is dead. There is no mercy here.

·   ·   ·   ·   ·

A week ago I am standing in my kitchen prepping breakfast when my phone rings. It is Igor, Jovina's husband, telling me that their daughter,

Elisa, has gone into premature labor. The baby had died early that morning. I clutch my own belly when I hear the news. I'm fourteen weeks pregnant myself. There is a sharp corner on the table in our kitchen that I always worry about when my young daughter comes running into the room. I press my thigh against it and summon pain, trying to keep my voice clear on the phone, trying to imagine what I can offer, what I can do. I try not to think of my own pregnancy. The sharp corner cuts deeper, and I hear Igor ask me to come to the hospital. And so I drop what I'm doing and go catch the bus. The hospital is reasonably close to our house, but it takes me more than an hour on an indirect bus route. I arrive at the large and imposing bus stop near the hospital and pass between all the vendors clustered with their plastic bags of nuts, cheap pens, and chewing gum slung over their shoulders, waiting to hop on a bus to sell these bits of affordable things to commuters. I call Igor again, but he doesn't answer. My head spins, and I vomit next to the bus stop before heading straight to the maternity wing.

I am directed to the postnatal ward by the nurse at the front desk. When I enter, I am momentarily stung by its cheerfulness—there are colorful balloons, large bouquets of flowers, and sweet Brazilian treats. The halls are filled with nurses, visiting families, and the sounds of new babies. Women and their babies move freely through the corridor. At first glance this is an uncomplicatedly happy place in a country that loves to love their children. There are oversized windows with no screens that stretch out like open walls between concrete abutments, and the sunshine from them fills the ward. The cement building makes the hundred-degree heat seem slightly cooler, but the ward is still sticky and uncomfortably hot. There is a long corridor and many bustling rooms. I try to maneuver through it all calmly, but my head is spinning. I was just at the hospital a few days ago for my first prenatal appointment. I approach the desk with my hushed voice of grief and whisper my request to see Elisa, the young woman whose baby has just died. I feel out of place here and also a bit embarrassed. Surely they will usher me to another floor. I must have made a mistake in being *here;* there must exist someplace tucked away from all this sunshine and life for a mother who just lost her child. Instead, I am directed down the hall to one of the large rooms. "On your right," says the nurse. She's kind but hurried.

I find Elisa in the first rod-metal bed in the room, pushed up against the concrete wall, almost tucked behind the door. There are five other beds in the room and a large window at the end of the room. There is an empty baby cot still next to her. Just an arm's length from her are five healthy mothers with days-old infants, crying, nursing, and sleeping. Elisa is lying in bed, recovering from her Cesarean in the post-op room for new mothers. She looks frail and tired. Jovina is there; we hug at the bedside. I sit down next to Elisa, and she tells me that her daughter, Megan, was born healthy. She was a few weeks early, but healthy. Then, this morning, Megan had become listless and died: "She was healthy and alive for a whole day!" Jovina cries. Jovina and Elisa bitterly explain that the doctors said Elisa had a urinary tract infection that went undetected, causing pre-term labor and Megan's eventual death. Elisa is speaking and crying loudly, her voice full of resentment and grief. They say the doctors betrayed them. Elisa had dutifully gone for all the checkups she could. It is the doctors' fault, Jovina cries, that they didn't notice there was something wrong when the baby was born.

Huddled at the bedside, Elisa and Jovina lack clear answers about *exactly* what has happened, what has led to Megan's death, but they understand that the doctors have laid the blame on Elisa rather than on any shortcoming of their own care and attention. The doctors told Elisa that had she had the urinary tract infection treated, this would not have happened. This won't change: years later much will remain uncertain about how Megan came to die so unexpectedly, and many questions will remain unanswered. I've never seen her medical charts, but the story is alarmingly predictable: the doctors unfold a tale that blames the mother, there is no discussion of lack of care and attention throughout her pregnancy or during the infant's short life, and there will be no meaningful follow-up. Elisa's daughter becomes another data point in the well-documented fact that Black infants die here at rates far higher than white infants. Yet the physicians were quick to blame Elisa: they distinctly implied that it was somehow all her fault; if she had done things differently, her daughter's death could have been avoided.

Elisa lies on the bed. Her body barely moves as she breathes. She barely registers our presence after she has told me what happened. But Jovina clutches my hands, her thumbs pressing into my wrists as she pulls my arms up over the bed so that we make a shaky arm bridge over Elisa. I'm reminded of the children's game, London Bridge Is Falling Down. I grip her tightly and the bridge holds. In her prayer she bemoans the doctors, but mostly she castigates this joke of a hospital, while assuring us that God has a plan for the future, even if this world seems intent on destroying it. If the doctors have failed them, Jesus will save. She asks for God to stay with Elisa and their entire family. She asks for God to be with them in the hospital. These words of prayer and reproach spill from her mouth. Like water from a drainpipe, these words spill all over Elisa. Submerged in her mother's prayers, she clings to the edges of the bed. Jovina begs Jesus for protection. I watch her try to hold back her own tears by tightening her upper body. Chest strong, she clenches my hands even more firmly, her nails cutting into my palms. We will not be broken by this, she promises Elisa. The prayer floods the room, and Jovina urges the angels to encircle Elisa's body and soul. I don't turn and face the other women in the room, but Jovina is praying so loudly that it would be impossible for these mothers to ignore the prayers, to ignore the death residing next to life. This is a prayer that shouts down the violence of death and raises up the promise of a better life with God. "Give me mercy," she cries.

When we leave, Jovina walks me down to the large atrium in the lobby, its angular shape constructed with heavy cement pillars. There Jovina takes my hands and begins to pray loudly to Jesus again. Jovina prays fervently, her body shaking while she does so. Embracing, we rock back and forth, and she murmurs her prayers for strength. At Elisa's bedside Jovina had been sad, but her prayers had been defiant. Here in the lobby, where Elisa can't see her, she breaks down. She almost falls to the floor, but I catch her in my arms. She cleaves to my body forcefully. She stops praying to Jesus, and she lifts her head to look me in the eyes. She howls like she is in physical pain: "This is life here, Laurie. You said you wanted to know. You said you wanted the book to be about life here. With certainty, this is life here."

This maternity ward is a dangerous place to be, and women know it. It is not uncommon for babies and laboring women to die here. Almost three years later, in July 2016, this same hospital became the center of a social-media firestorm when another premature infant was removed from the ICU and taken off oxygen support because the bed space was needed by a different premature infant. According to a doctor who explained the action, the infant removed from oxygen support was deemed the healthiest of the group of babies in ICU and was put in a regular ward without round-the-clock care. There he developed an infection and died within two days, after he had lived for fifty-six days in the ICU on oxygen support. The family said that the infant died while they were not there. No one noticed. They found him dead in his cot hours after his death. The father, in response, punched a hospital door, shattering its glass. The hospital, in response, called the police, and the family now finds themselves in debt from a fine levied for damaging public property. The story did not become a flashpoint because of its extraordinariness, though. Rather, hundreds of commenters on social media flooded the site with their own similar stories. What made it so unnerving was that at almost the exact same time as this occurred—minus a day or two—Mayor Eduardo Paes of Rio de Janeiro visited the same hospital to inaugurate the opening of the hospital's new emergency facility. For many this was simply too much, a clear and demoralizing demonstration of the selective presence and absence of the state and the ubiquity of violence that unfolds on women's and children's bodies within these state-run spaces that is always somehow unremarkable and never acted on.[1]

CARVING OUT EVANGELICAL SPACE

On the hillside Jovina and I continue to stare out over the city. To me prayers feel like an inadequate response to the loss and ensuing grief, but Jovina still calls her prayers out to the sky. Her body tilts over the hillside, but, like the boulder, she remains grounded. The prayers don't carry her away today. They lift nothing of the load she carries. I've never seen her so vulnerable. She's always been more awake than most, full of that tough stuff people always remark on in people. She is caring and generous, and fragile too. The loss doubled her over in the hospital lobby, striking her in her gut, and she has not been the same since. We send our prayers out over the hilltop, out and up into the city, pleading sounds carried into open windows, across motorways, up into the heavens. When we descend, Jovina clutches my hand, and we hold tight to each other as we maneuver the loose rocks amid the rough and steep decline of our path. The boulder remains on the hillside, a keeper of prayers, of hope, loss, desire, resentment, and love, eroding at a pace we cannot see. Jovina returns night after night to the rock, her prayers carving out a way to live in this world. I too will return here again and again over the course of my own pregnancy. Despite myself, I'll pray on the rock with Jovina, reminding God that we are here.

.   .   .   .   .

I come up the road, around the corner, and find Jovina working in her small family-owned restaurant attached to her home. It is two weeks after Megan's death, and Elisa is back home again. Jovina is busy with customers, so I sit on the open patio and wait for her to have a break. It is mostly all family and Evangelical friends dining here and not a large crowd. At a lull Jovina comes up to me. She does not want to chat; she urges me to go upstairs to visit with Elisa, saying there is a service going on upstairs that I should join. I go up the steep flight of stairs to the one-room apartment over the restaurant. I find Jovina's aunt and uncle and her cousins. They are praying over Elisa's body as she lies in bed, staring up at the ceiling with wide-open eyes.

Elisa's aunt falls to her knees, her bones clunking against the hard ground. My eyes focus on her bare knees against the rough floor. Her body shakes with a prayer for Jesus, and I watch the way her knees scratch the floor, her arms lifted to the sky as the sand and grit of the floor needle her delicate skin. On her knees, bedside the bed, she asks for mercy for her niece, her brother's youngest daughter, who has just lost her first child, a daughter. She doesn't ask for meaning, just mercy, not a conclusion but at least a pause, a breath, a period, a stone to rest on.

Elisa's aunt stands up tall now. Her legs stretched, knees unlocked, she raises herself on tiptoe. With her hands in the air, she shouts and commands. "Jesus," she calls, "come and hold Elisa." "*Elisa!*" she calls, "hear Jesus at the window." My eyes dart to the pulled curtains that block the afternoon heat. Elisa's aunt, uncle, and two cousins all hold hands over her bed. These are her family and friends, her congregation. Congregating now, they beg Jesus to enter the house and heal Elisa, to wash Elisa of her sins and bring her back to this life. They say, "We know that Megan is with you and will live forever with you." They pray that Elisa might hear Jesus's voice, and they tell Elisa that she can tell Jesus the truth, any truth, and that Jesus will hear her truth and love her no matter what. I have been sitting on the sofa until this moment, but they insist I join in the prayer. I grasp hands and become part of the circle around the bedside. The prayers last more than an hour, as each person in the circle takes turns asking for blessings, healing, mercy, a route out of pain. Elisa, lying in bed the whole time, barely acknowledges us. From time to time, though, she will reach up and grip a hand in the circle, tying herself up in this knot of prayer.

Suddenly, Elisa's uncle calls out for angels; he asks for angels to fill the space and bring their power and protection. He chants as he calls for them, the lilt of his prayer and call finding a beat that rocks him on his feet, bouncing through the room. "Angels, angels, *angels!* Angels, angels, *angels!* Angels, angels, *angels!*"

I find myself chanting it too. Later I try to capture its rhythm in my field notes, as it bounces through my body all afternoon, even years later. I try to note the way the chant pulsed and moved, reverberated, called up. What tools do we have for rhythmic notation?

"Angels, angels, *angels!* Angels, angels, *angels!* Angels, angels, *angels!*"

When her family finishes praying, they kiss Elisa on her forehead and descend the stairs to the restaurant. Meanwhile, I sit on the bed and touch Elisa's shoulder. She rolls toward me and puts her hand in mine.

MOURNING THE UNMOURNABLE

Elisa stays in bed for months, listless with grief and depression. I return to Elisa almost every afternoon and often arrive while different Evangelical groups come to pray over her. These prayer groups are mostly organized by Elisa's aunt, Nina, who is a pastor in her own home-based Evangelical congregation. She started her own church with her husband, and they currently rent out a small space for services in their community on Friday nights when they can afford it. Nina visits daily, bringing with her other family members and parishioners who can pray for Elisa while she recovers. They grip her tightly as she lies on the bed; they pray over her body.

They come each day and ask God for peace, for both Elisa and for Megan. They pray for Jesus to hold Elisa through this trauma. They chant for angels to support her. They are the angels that support her. They don't seem to expect Elisa to respond or participate. They are not waiting for her to rise out of bed and sing God's praises, Nina tells me one afternoon, after many afternoons together, when I dare to question the point of all this out loud. "Our prayers secure Elisa," she tells me. "We want her to know that Jesus loves her and that God has the answers to all of this. She doesn't have to be strong. Jesus will be strong for her." She's matter-of-fact about it. She knows what she knows.

In chapter 5 I return to this bedside and cover the rumors that circulated about Elisa and the loss of her infant daughter. The rumors were cruel and called into question how Megan died and who might be to blame. The believers who showed up daily supported Elisa materially, financially, and emotionally, even when they'd heard the rumors and, most likely, believed them. For months they brought generous gifts of food. They even raised money through a collection to pay for follow-up visits in a private health-care facility so she wouldn't have to return to the public system. Much later on they still showed up, to celebrate and support her new relationships and the children she would go on to have in years to come. But while she lay in bed, vulnerable, they also demanded that she speak with Jesus, heavily intoning that she could tell Jesus anything, that Jesus would forgive all. Their prayers, it seemed to me, were also condemnations, meant to urge Elisa toward Jesus and the forgiveness they so desired for her.

On that first day, I stay late with Elisa, long after her aunt leaves and the prayers end. We watch cartoons and drink warm *nescau* (a hot chocolate drink) on her double bed positioned in the living room, in front of the television. I make up the *nescau* on the little gas stove in the kitchen and lay out a plate of cookies too. This is the bed she has shared with her sister for most of her life, and just a foot away—close enough that you could reach out and touch someone in it—is her mother and father's bed. There is no couch; it was removed to make room for the baby's crib. The crib is large, US American–style. Elisa had asked me to purchase one for her in the Zona Sul, so I'd arranged for it to be delivered as a baby shower gift. After Megan's death I asked Jovina if I should arrange for the crib to be removed before Elisa returned home from the hospital. I was worried that

Elisa might not want it to be in the house as it would be the first thing she would see when she returned home. My offer, while received generously, was dismissed: "We have no need to forget Megan," Jovina explained.

In the days following Megan's death, community public-health agents also came to visit. "They came once," Elisa tells me. "You missed them." They updated and then closed her pregnancy file, she said, leaving no open file for baby Megan, no vaccines to give, no healthy weight checks, no feeding advice. No one had much to say about their visit. They had closed the file and left. The chasm in responses was clear to everyone. Judith Butler (2006) argues that precarious life is the ungrievable life. Butler's position is in sync with others who have charted the diverse ways that power is mobilized against those unambiguously excluded and left to die. Precarious life is marked by terms that define the grievability of death, where rituals of grief and mourning are boundary markers that determine what kind of lives and deaths are valuable. The state-run hospital—which failed Elisa and Megan in almost every possible and substantial way—certainly conceived of Megan's life as ungrievable. There is, quite literally, no space—built, moral, or otherwise—where the state might mourn her death. Megan's death was treated as unexceptional and mundane. The responsibility to love and support Elisa and the space to grieve Megan would have to be created at home, in the churches, at the bedside, and through God, family, and faith above all. It was easier to call on angels than to believe the community-health agents would provide some kind of care that mattered. Megan and Elisa's family and Evangelical community gave voice to the conditions of life and death and faith. Through their prayer work, through showing up, through material and spiritual practice, they sought to hold on to Megan and carry Elisa through her storm. They grieved the baby.

Before Megan's birth Elisa had already tattooed Megan's name on her leg in an elegant cursive script. She had revealed this at her baby shower, just a few weeks before Megan's birth and death. In the pictures I took that day, Elisa's big pregnant belly sticks out between her youthful cheetah-print spandex leggings and her black crop top. In the pictures she is young and healthy and smiling, with her braces—a big purchase she had saved for—catching the light. We had gathered outside her house, hung balloons, prepared a diaper cake, and devoured a table-sized *bolo de salgado* (a savory cake made of ham, olives, corn, and beets and iced with

mayonnaise) that everyone on the street and surrounding area could par-
take in. There are other blurry pictures of us writing "MEGAN" on her belly
with lipstick. We'd painted a beaming sun around her belly button. The
shower was modest, but, as the sun set over us, we had danced and laughed
in the street. Elisa had shown us the tattoo that night, already so proud of
her first child, not yet born.

Later she would add both the dates of Megan's birth and death to her tattoo. Elisa's sister and brother did the same, as did Megan's father. Each tattooed Megan's name on their bodies. One afternoon, just a few weeks after
Megan's death, Elisa's brother pulls me aside to show me his newest tattoo.
It's a climbing water lily, with a woman growing out of it. The flower and the
woman look like they are dancing together in the water, moving easily with
the current up his arm. The new tattoo covers up an old one. He tells me that
at his next session he'll be getting a tattoo of Megan's name added to it. He
adds, "What happened was a mess—but she is with God now."

On Elisa's sister's shoulder, Megan's name will be tattooed, joining a list
of all the other children in the family: Megan will live on in this informal
census with her cousins, binding the dead to the living in one of a myriad
of ways. Elisa's sister will pierce her skin with a needle and ink, reconfigur-
ing skin as both monument and census to life and death; she will mourn
the unmournable on her body. Megan continues to be openly grieved,
prayed for in church services, commemorated on social media, and celebrated in annual ceremonies. We will grieve openly for a long time—more
than a year—for Megan. We will mark her six-month birthday, and then,
at what would have been her first birthday, we will celebrate her short life
at an Evangelical service in her cousin's home with a beautiful pink-frosted
cake to share. We gather for her, knowing the future is on its way, even if
the contours of that future are unknowable and, sometimes quite literally,
not of this world.

LANDSCAPES OF EVANGELICALISM IN THE WESTERN *SUBÚRBIOS*

Below the rock on the hill, Jovina and I move through the streets together,
walking back to where I live. We have lived in the community of Batan, in

the western *subúrbios* of Rio de Janeiro, for just under three years. I was
a new mother when we moved there: my daughter, Arden, was just one at
the time. Because she was still prone to hang from me wherever I went,
people initially called me "the mother of the blonde" rather than by my
name. Then, in the last eight months of living there, I was pregnant with
my son, Jude. My partner, Graham, lived with us too, commuting between
Rio and São Paulo for his own research, doing shift work with the police
at the time.

It had been hard to find a place to live in Batan. We had met the owners
during lunch at a local restaurant, where they had explained that they had
a place they wanted to rent out, but they didn't have the money to complete the unfinished roof over the kitchen. It was a three-story building
close to a main square, with four families living on the first two floors. The
roof had fallen in and needed to be rebuilt, and there was some additional
structural work and plumbing that needed to be done as well. These people we'd met over lunch owned just the third floor and had lived there
before the pacification intervention had reorganized the community. They
had moved out to a quieter street when the pacification force arrived.
They suggested that if we had the money to pay for the repairs up front,
we could rent it for as long as we'd like. We visited the house and met the
other families living in the building. Graham and I chatted and decided
we trusted these people we had just met over lunch, and so we arranged to
give them the money for the repairs and crossed our fingers it would all
work out. A few days later we returned and gave them approximately
US$1,000—a huge sum of money for both them and us. The repairs hap-
pened swiftly once they could afford the material costs. We moved in just
over a month later, with few delays.

The people we'd met for lunch, and given the thousand dollars to, were
Jovina and Igor. They would go from landlords to dear friends, guides, and
collaborators. I think back regularly on how we just happened to start
chatting, how we hit it off, and how we knew right away that each of us
was worth the risk, that we had a sense about one another as trustworthy.
I'd felt it in my gut. Jovina says, it was—with certainty—God's plan.

Stories circulate about Jovina's family and the timing of their move out
of the house we would later rent. People say her eldest son, João Vitor, is a
member of the armed group that was forced out by the militia of off-duty

police officers and firefighters that controlled the community before a state-led pacification project occupied Batan. Jovina's family moved to the outskirts of town just before this happened, and her son has since built a small business selling perfume, cologne, and running shoes. He's a believer now too and goes to church multiple times per week. João Vitor and his girlfriend, Rafaela, a college student studying to become a pharmacist, became good friends of mine, and I attended Rafaela's baptism. Our families had all traveled together on a church-organized bus trip to a small farm with a pool—farther west, away from the city—and spent the day together in celebration, with a big barbeque and a football match. The day ended with Rafaela and many others from their congregation stepping into the pool to be baptized in front of their family and friends. A small choir sang on the pool deck as the pastor led the service from the shallow end.

In the beginning, when I first moved to Batan, I had been curious about how members of the nonstate group Amigos dos Amigos had been pushed out by a militia of off-duty police officers and firefighters and then about what had happened to those police and firefighters when the state-led policing force—the pacification force—had commanded control of the community. João Vitor made clear that my notion of divisions between these groups as clear-cut, and even knowable, was faulty. In his former house João Vitor showed me how the doorbell had ADA—the initials of the trafficking group—carved into it. It was the highest building on the street, with clear views into Fumacê, a neighboring public-housing block controlled by a different trafficking group. The exterior walls were riddled with bullet holes. He had picked up and moved to the far edges of Batan sometime in November 2006, right around the time the militia took control, supposedly violently forcing out the traffickers. João Vitor explained that he was and wasn't forced out. He lived on the edge of Batan, and he maintained his community connections, showing up to the houses of families in need with twenty-pound bags of rice. His role in the community had been muted by the militia, but he had not been violently forced out. The militia did not embrace him, but he was allowed to exist as a supportive and exemplary community figure. Now that he was a believer, of course, he moved even more freely through the community.

Evangelicalism in Latin American has been conceived as a kind of strategy for maneuvering the complex political and social landscape of violence, often linked to attempts to leave criminal organizations. I could try to make sense of João Vitor's story in this way. But to conceptualize conversion as just a route out of gang membership is potentially reductive. The violence that trafficking causes in many men's lives—and in the lives of their families—makes Evangelicalism appealing, but it is not fair to say their conversions are directly linked or, worse, farcically linked to a route out of trafficking. Their conversions, as Kevin O'Neill (2015) tracks, are always also aspirational and heartfelt modes of healing.[2]

Besides, men like João Vitor and their families were intent on showing me something different about their communities: retraining my eye to what they thought mattered in the first place. For many in the community, the logic of pacification simply continued the logic of the militia, which had for the most part been the logic of the traffickers. The idea, then, of marking time as before and after pacification made little sense for many in the neighborhood. People even balked at my attempts to know the community through an attention to agents of security, and they were both careful and direct about pointing this out to me. Another close friend in the community cut me off early in my research: "Why are you asking all these questions about pacification? . . . The UPP [pacification force] is the best of them all, but they are all the same. I don't know about the UPP and what is better or not better. It is not my choice for the UPP to be here—traffickers, militia, UPP—these are all the same choices. Only God knows, Laurie. Only God knows our future." And even more to the point: "Why do you keep saying 'life in a pacified favela'? . . . We don't live in a UPP, we live with God!"

This neighbor, along with Jovina, Elisa, and João Vitor, are each part of a growing Evangelicalism that has altered the religious terrain of Brazil over the past few decades. Jovina had grown up in the northeast of Brazil and had found Jesus when she was first pregnant with João Vitor and her marriage had become violent. She had found Jesus during a moment when she had never felt weaker. Her husband eventually found Jesus too, and they built a home together in the rapidly expanding suburbs of Rio in the early 1980s, following their Evangelical networks across the country. Believers often move from Evangelical communities in the northeast to Evangelical communities in Rio and often move their children among Evangelical families for temporary stays as they sort out housing and employment. Jovina had previously rented out the house she owns to various Evangelical families that she had met through Evangelical networks that stretch from São Luís do Maranhão to Rio. Still today believers help their Evangelical community to buy the cross-country bus tickets they need to move to Rio (or back north). As believers journey across the country, Evangelical networks provide money, shelter, childcare, and work opportunities up and down the country.

In Batan the kinds and forms of Evangelicalism practiced are rarely linked to just one branch of Pentecostalism or one formal church.[3] Many, like Jovina, identify first and foremost as *crentes* (believers) or simply Evangelicos (Evangelicals). Most don't attend just one kind of Pentecostal or neo-Pentecostal church. While many attend an Assembly of God or an IURD service one night a week, much worship occurs in smaller congregations without any formal affiliation to a well-known and established Pentecostal Church. These churches depend on large, extended families and networks of friends to support them, and people move around to different churches in these networks throughout the week. These services take place in improvised churches made in rented storefronts or inside family homes, where living rooms have been converted to sanctuaries. Families host their own services in their homes, inviting a pastor to give a service, renting a sound system for an evening to broadcast music and sermons out to the street, and collecting chairs from other households to accommodate everyone in their living rooms and outside on front stoops. Like the path followed by Elisa's aunt, becoming a pastor is a calling to minister to those most in need, without a formal church or religious organization to confirm the role. That is Jesus's job, they would say.

Elisa's aunt and uncle had started their small Evangelical congregation in the community of Vila Vintém, attracting many parishioners by openly sharing their past experiences with violence in their marriage and then their conversion. Elisa's uncle said it was shame that first led him to Jesus: "Shame. It was always shame. The Catholic Church shamed me. I beat my wife and my children every night. In the Catholic Church I was shamed for this, and I couldn't talk about it. In the Evangelical Church I was loved for it. Jesus loved me even though I beat my wife. Jesus still called my name and asked me to join him. He called me while I was beating her, and one night I answered him." They each recounted this story often. His wife told me that Jesus had entered their house, taking her husband in his arms and telling him that he loved him. I also heard this story through his preaching. From the small, raised stage in front of his congregation, he told and retold this story of unconditional acceptance and redemption. His violent past was not whispered in hushed voices but shouted and celebrated. His leadership was in many ways even premised on this. "Jesus sought me out, Laurie," he said. For João Vitor—his nephew—this was a powerful lesson. Learning that Jesus's love extended to him not just in spite of his shame and failures but because of them was central to his own conversion, he explained.

On Friday nights the church services and preparations light up the streets of Batan and surrounding communities. These services often last three to four hours and are followed by a homemade meal, soda pop, and cake, passed around on crinkly plastic plates, disposable cups, and small paper napkins. Children who typically race the streets in shorts and T-shirts walk carefully in their finest clothes to services that start as the light fades. The fluorescent lights of competing churches flood the streets, as the loudspeakers pump the pastors' voices into the roads, their voices calling on Jesus. Echoing through the streets, they shout down the demons that they say have cluttered up people's lives: betrayal, greed, and anger, taking material form through adultery, alcohol consumption, or violence. These services are always charismatic events with singing and prayer. They often include exorcisms of the demons that believers say haunt and prey on people, the demons that have weaseled their way into lives to corrupt from the inside out are fought off in near-violent battles during services.

·   ·   ·   ·   ·

I grasp Jovina's arm as we step out of the hills and back into the street. We maneuver around a sinkhole that emerged at the street that abutted my own. A few months ago the road had simply given way, opening into a gaping hole, large enough to swallow a whole car. People had collected some old chairs and rope to mark it off, so cars and people knew to swerve around. Peering down into it, we joke that it might be connected to a series of police tunnels. Really, it's just another bit of proof that we live somewhere that doesn't matter much to anyone who has power or money to wield. It had rained heavily a few nights earlier, and the sinkhole now holds enough water to be a drowning hazard. Tonight, as we walk back from our prayers on the hillside, we chat with people as they walk home or linger on their front verandas. My house had flooded in the rains too. The water had come tumbling through our ceiling, flooding our shared staircase in the multistory, multifamily home we live in. The water levels had risen in the streets because the sewer systems were inadequately designed and clogged with uncollected garbage. As the water rose to the height of an adult knee, it swelled into people's homes, saturating everything from mattresses to refrigerators. One Evangelical friend reminded me of a common saying, however, as she laid her daughter's crib mattress out in the sunshine the next day to dry: "Se Deus mandou essa tempestade, ele sabe que seu barco é forte o bastante para não naufragar" (If God sends a storm, he knows his ship is strong enough not to be shipwrecked). Here the image of the storm is not meant to be menacing but rather a signal of strength. In the western suburbs there is no doubt that storms—of all varieties—will at some point come for you. But God would guide you to calm waters, Evangelicals would say: "You would never be shipwrecked if you believed. Your boat would sail on as the storm ravages." "God knows all," they remind us, explaining that their lives and futures have never been in the hands of anyone but a grace-filled God, lifting them up when everything else is busy tearing them down.

AVOWING GOD, NOT RIGHTS

Much writing on Rio, and Brazil more broadly, has carefully considered how abandonment and precarity subsume the conditions of life for the poor and marginalized. Such descriptions have been developed by scholars of Brazil, who have detailed the very particular conditions here, specifically the ways precarity often hinges on and is enforced by entrenched inequalities.

The Evangelicals I worked with throughout my research both live with and acknowledge the ways that the state seems intent on destroying them, in actions both direct and indirect. Yet they insist on a hopeful future in almost everything they do, whether they conceive of that future existing in this world or another. That hope, however, is rarely hinged on political success. It is not a hope premised through a politics of resistance or insurgence, a demand made on the state, or the right to be included and recognized in the city.[4] Rarely did I see Evangelicals seek or desire justice from the state or talk through modes of state reparation or the extension of rights. Rather, more often than not, I saw people engage in a politics of avowal, a politics that insisted on affirming their worth and value, on affirming the existence of grace in the city guaranteed by a God who knows, with little regard for whether the state and its actors might agree or not. For many the Evangelical promise of salvation has reorganized the ways they experience the cruel and rampant conditions of abandonment.

A politics of avowal is an insistence that they have *already* been saved. Their Evangelical faith was never described to me as something like an escape hatch. Rather, in various ways, it was depicted as a form of knowledge about the truth, merit, and eventuality of their promised futures. They *knew* their worth and their children's worth, their place in the kingdom of heaven. They carve and mold these futures and make new possible worlds through experiences of prayer and faith. In a world that does not bend to them but makes them bend to it, they insist on other spaces that hold them, cradle them, and love them and their children. Here Evangelical forms of grieving and togetherness were a way to redefine the conditions of life and death, a way to envision new possibilities for life and its value. In mourning Megan as they did, they insisted on a politics of life much larger than any politics of this earth, city, or suburb.

2 Disinfectant

The density of the fragrance lands on our lips. They curl. We smell it as we breathe, the odors lodging themselves in our nostril membranes, coating the delicate scroll-shaped bones that make up the human nose. Milene, a devout Evangelical believer, purrs a short prayer in response to the rising fumes. Half of Milene's body disappears into a big blue fifty-five-gallon barrel of thick, liquid fragrance. She draws a large scoop with a spouted jug she has cut from the bottom third of an old plastic bottle and then appears again. She pours the liquid gently through a funnel, also repurposed, down some green plastic tubing. The viscous, bright-white substance seems to move lazily down the tube, and at times Milene has to coax it by jiggling the hose or whispering a little prayer of encouragement. The plastic tubing feeds the fragrance into a reused soda bottle that we have already filled with one part water and one part bleach. The first steps—filling the bottles with bleach and water—are easier, as bleach and water are cheap and plentiful. It's the fragrance we don't want to lose a drop of. Milene is careful and practiced in her movements, and this morning we do not lose any of the fragrance in transfer. Its strong fumes swirl, burning my eyes and nose. The smell coats our tongues, where fragrance mingles with spit, so that we taste it.

We are tucked into a small workshop, accessible only through the kitchen, in Milene's self-constructed house in a small community in the western *suburbios* of Rio de Janeiro. We are making a fragrant disinfectant for household cleaning that Milene and her family sell in Evangelical-owned shops in surrounding communities. With more than two hundred bottles of disinfectant stacked as high as our waists, Milene speaks to the fragrance as if it were an embodied form. She speaks to it in a kind of gentle religious oratory, substantially more reticent than a typical Charismatic prayer. She coaxes it lightly, as you might speak to a small child in need of gentle encouragement. As the fragrance moves along, she exhales and whispers, "This is *divino* [divine]." Then Milene passes one end of the tube to me while pinching the other. In a quick move she pops the lid on the top of the bottle and shakes vigorously. Here she agitates it all together: fragrance, bleach, water, prayer, breath.

We do not wear gloves as we bottle, and even a little bit of liquid on the skin burns. I ask Milene if she has ever thought of looking for different, more secure work, maybe work in the *centro?* "No," she responds sharply, giving me a strange look. She takes another deep breath of fragrance. "This fragrance is given by God," she says. "These things God sets in our path are divine. God is our cradle. This work is me in God's arms."

Milene's rebuke of my question and her defiant assertion that the liquid fragrance is a gift from God seems at odds with what she knows I already know about the fragrance. What we are mixing is a waste product taken from the factory of a well-known international fragrance and flavor company, with multiple billions of dollars in global sales annually, strategically placed in Rio's *suburbios*. Milene's husband, Enzo, works the graveyard shift mixing perfume, and he occasionally and surreptitiously removes the discarded fragrance waste after his shift ends. If Enzo was slightly unsure about the arrangement, Milene knew straight away what he had uncovered. For when Milene smelled it, she was without doubt: it was *pedaços de graça*, (pieces of grace)—God's grace set in their path, a means to construct a future.

It was also highly concentrated: only a tiny amount of this fragrance is ever used in a small bottle of perfume, meaning that the hundreds of gallons the couple has on hand could be used to make tens of thousands of individual bottles of perfume. Milene's fragrant disinfectant deftly moves through the *suburbios*, desired by many: the waste flows outside the factory, is poured into bottles, and then reaches people's homes through tight-knit Evangelical networks. It is perhaps not surprising that intimacy with God would occur here in the form of a popular, fragrant cleaning disinfectant. Scent is not trivial in the *suburbios:* this piece of Rio's map is often defined by its lack of cleanliness. Acute water shortages plague the neighborhoods, and they are without basic material infrastructures. Indeed, in Rio de Janeiro and other cities in Brazil, the term *suburbio*, like *favela*, represents not just a deficiency of infrastructure and services but also references the Black people who live in them. Historically, and still today, the larger society understands these communities as racially inferior. The people who live there are described as immoral and unclean in both character and body.[1]

A story about Evangelicalism, margins, smells, and soaps—put to work to construct a powerful disinfectant—is part of a larger story of the spatial and racial politics and temporalities of the city and also an alternative story, a story centered less on history and the present-day landscape of destruction and containment and more as an elaboration of life, space, and joy. What enables something like repurposed waste to become "pieces of grace"—a divinely given fragrance—is a project of grace in the city, both bestowed and created. Here a political project of grace concerns how people elaborate their desires—for goodness and safety, honor, value, and ethics—into land-scapes through concrete and fences and disinfectant certainly but also through shared dreams, visions, and sensations: a graceful elaboration.

·   ·   ·   ·   ·

Milene and Enzo each came to Batan separately but were both originally from São Luís do Maranhão, in the northeast of Brazil. They came by bus on multiday trips, passing through the center of Rio, before heading west down the coast, not north through the interior highway, Avenida Brasil. Their buses all stopped just outside City of God, the favela made infamous by the internationally acclaimed film of the same name. This path they took was taken by many before them too. From the 1970s to 1990s, City of God was the gateway to all the western nodes of the city. You could eas-ily catch a bus into the interior of Rio de Janeiro State from here, winding your way through roads that weave in and around the mountains that divide the west from the south. It was around this time that elite and middle-class Rio residents started to move westward down the coast into the Barra de Tijuca. That shift generated a large construction boom that required cheap physical and domestic labor. The many migrants moving from Brazil's northeast at this time did not move to centrally located favelas in Rio but instead started to build their own homes and communities on land near these construction sites.[2]

As a child, Milene had lived on a small island off the coast of São Luís with almost no contact with anyone but her family and a few neighbors. They lived on the island without a boat and no permanent access to the mainland. On a research trip to São Luís, I met with Milene's older sister, who explained to me that, when Milene was little, she had broken her foot so badly that her foot twisted upward and sat next to her knee. With no boat to take them to the mainland to seek care, Milene had endured the pain for over a month, until a boat happened by and her father arranged for them to travel with the boaters to seek medical assistance at a small missionary clinic on the mainland. When I asked Milene about this story, she said it was confirmation of "God's grace." She insisted that the man with the boat had actually been an Evangelical pastor and that it was due to her mother's Evangelical faith that the pastor had even stopped at their small island to minister to them.

When Milene moved to Rio de Janeiro, she was singularly focused on moving in step with her Evangelical community. It didn't matter to her if infrastructure was shabby, if drug-trafficking groups governed, or if there were nearby hospitals. What mattered was whether there was a strong Evangelical community that would offer an enduring connection and support. From this base of support, both Milene and Enzo could envision for themselves a life of possibility.

Milene and Enzo now live in a house they constructed themselves from the ground up. As we bottle disinfectant together, her own children and the neighborhood little ones peek into the back room, asking me where my daughter is; they want her to come out and play. Milene yells at them to leave the room and to get back outside. The kids slink out of the room and find their older brother; they taunt and dare him to dole out *açaí* from the little shop that Milene's daughter-in-law runs. They recently put together the money to convert the front room into a shop, where they sell hamburgers at night and *acaí* during the day. This made the living room smaller but was worth the gamble for the possibility of extra income. Off the bottling room is the kitchen, which has two bedrooms connected to it. One bedroom is for Milene and Enzo and the second bedroom is for all the children and Ana. The room for the children has four single mattresses pushed together on the floor. There is a tangle of sheets and blankets draped across the beds and another sheet that hangs from the ceiling and functions as a door.

Houses—like disinfectant—are carefully pieced together with gifts from God too. Milene and Enzo, like most people here, first put down a solid foundation for their house, then continued to build up and out over the years, buying supplies when they could afford them and collecting discarded materials that could be repurposed. The corrugated asbestos roofing tiles were lifted and cut by the couple, reused each time another story was added. There are windows that look into other rooms rather than outdoors, a reminder that new rooms have been added over time. Each step on the cement staircase has a slightly different discoloration, a visual representation of the years that passed between the time that each step was built as well as the different materials used at different moments. Like the fragrance, building materials—rummaged, collected, recycled—all come to them as gifts from God.

Milene insists that God's grace can appear in material form, through bits and pieces, set down in their path to prosperity. God can—and does—manifest in margins. A bag of cement (no small thing) claimed from a work site at a discount, Enzo tells me, is a gift from God. These are not miracle gifts—*a brand new car!*—but instead little bits of things, often bought second- or thirdhand or discarded, found, and reclaimed. Grace is found in pieces. Christians at the margins use the margins to get by. These pieces, of course, are parts of global-supply chains, pieces that generate hundreds of millions of dollars, flowing from Rio to London, Rio to New York, with real material effects. The suburbs of Rio are not distant from center finances but integral to them. They are often containers for industrial practices and cheap labor that do not belong *materially* in the center, even if their finances do.

.   .   .   .   .

I move down the highway with Milene's son, Roger, in his small white van, a three-seater Fiat. He saved to buy the secondhand truck and now runs his own van delivery service. He hatched a plan with a local bakery to deliver bread throughout the city. He now collects the ubiquitous Brazilian breakfast rolls in bulk from a large suburban bakery and delivers throughout the center. Their main client is a large catering firm that provides meals for private hospitals in the Zona Sul. Suburban bread travels down the highway in the early morning hours, off to nourish the elite as they seek private care. I know that one of Roger's stops is a nice bakery in the enclave community Santa Teresa, a beautiful hilltop space, popular with tourists in the city. I ask him if I can have an early-morning ride the next day, as I want to visit a friend who lives there. He warns me that Santa Teresa is one of his last stops, and he laughs at my improbable choice of transport. In the end he welcomes the company; my curiosity is always a good story for later on, he laughs. So we move with pieces of bread up Avenida Brasil.

Even in the early-morning hours, the highway hums, full of lights, though the congestion is far less than it would be in the daytime. We move down the large highway artery that links the suburbs to the center, passing the industries that have built the suburbs as we know them. We pass the Guadalupe housing complex, one of the largest public-housing blocks in the city, which dominates the skyline here. It was built in the 1960s—part of a larger project designed to remove unwanted people from the city. Guadalupe was built as part of mass eradication and displacement efforts that saw many historically Black communities forcibly displaced from centrally located favelas and relocated to poorly constructed housing blocks or plots in the *suburbios* (Leeds 1974; McCann 2014, 12). This attempt to "cleanse" the center of racialized "marginals" was often done under the auspices of locating these far-flung communities to something akin to idealized US suburbs (Perlman 1976). Indeed, historical public-health and urban-planning projects in Brazil were often attempts at alleviating the city from the "blight" of Blackness and its accompanying smells, flavors, and presentations.[3]

Race in Rio is constructed and experienced in infinite ways but is at least partly linked to the sensorial constructions of people, places, and homes. This becomes obvious when we consider that whiteness in Rio is almost always rendered as sensorially neutral or blank. Removals, then, are always part of aspirational projects to reconfigure Rio into what elites imagine London or Paris to be: white, clean, and orderly. Rather than a diseased port city defined by squalor, they desire a clean Rio defined by a project of *branqueamento* (whitening), which means not just skin color but also a way of being in the world, an aesthetic produced through architectures, political sensibilities, modes of leisure, and tempos.[4] It means waking up in the morning at a reasonable hour and going for a stroll to your local bakery, where fresh bread is hot and ready for you—or, better yet, awaking to your maid having already purchased the bread. The temporality of whiteness is fueled through invisible labor, an unseen and unknown van that moves up and down the highway, with cheap bread from the suburbs ready to be sold at triple the price in chic bakeries.

Nearby we pass a large compound that used to distribute and ship asbestos. It has since changed hands and no longer trades in the newly banned material, chrysotile asbestos, which has been tied to deadly mesothelioma and other diseases. But for years it stood there, a major source of employment for many in the area. Asbestos afterlives linger, however, as asbestos roofing tiles are still used, often in self-constructed housing projects in the suburbs. For Milene and Enzo, each time another story is added to their home, they reuse the same asbestos sheets. After heavy rains Enzo will climb to the rooftop to rearrange the sheets, patching them where necessary.

Next we approach the flavor and fragrance factory where Enzo works. These industries and trade centers follow in the footsteps of previous generations of factory works relegated to the suburbs. The spatial formations of Rio's *subúrbios*, colloquially characterized as "informal sprawl," actually emerge from calculated practices by companies to have their workers build homes on factory land and then extract rent from them (Fischer 2008; McCann 2014). This practice of building on factory land—or very close by—was part of the informal and underregulated real-estate and land-title market that overwhelmingly disfavored Black Brazilians. In the early 1900s the western suburbs were dominated by the textile industries, and workers and their families were forced to pay rent to live on the land owned by the mills. As Teresa Meade explains, this resulted in families essentially trapped and isolated on suburban textile mill lands, unable to organize more broadly across the city to demand better pay and rights (1997, 56). And, while the suburbs were the fastest-growing sections of Rio between 1890 and 1920, growing by 100 percent in that period, city officials did not conceive of them as part of the city (71).

Moving through the city with Roger, then, chatting together about our children, faith, and work—and transporting bread—we move through landscapes defined largely by their ability to extract and harm. These are wastelands contained from the center. I'm reminded (again) of how residents must work and live in the interstices, infectiousness, and abrasions of chronic industrial pollution, toxicity, and faulty infrastructures, giving way to ideas and demands for disinfectant. In this terrain disinfectant—both a concept and a divine material good—becomes a key way to reckon with everyday environmental and political governance. Paying attention to a divine disinfectant—what it is meant to clean up and obscure—seems important. A politics of disinfectant is a way to think about how individuals and households negotiate and live alongside toxic environmental leakage in everyday life, making and finding grace among the discarded.

I pop out of the truck in Santa Teresa, kissing Roger on the cheek. My white body blends into the landscape here with ease. "Blessings to you," Roger shouts to me, as he drives away. Of course, I will see him later that night. His kids will climb my stairs looking for my daughter; they will invite her to play. I'll dole out paper and markers and juice. I move through the city unencumbered, neutral.

THE SCENT OF GRACE

It is a hot morning, and the sun is relentless. February is nearing its end; carnival was over two weeks ago. Most of the revelry that has carried us this far through the summer weather, when the temperature peaks above one hundred degrees Fahrenheit, is gone. It is now just a long trek until the hot weather begins to dissipate into the rains of March. The air is not humid; instead, a dry wind is caught in the valley, caused by moist air being pushed from the Atlantic over the mountain pass that separates the western *subúr-bios* from the ocean. For this reason this and the surrounding communities are the hottest spots in the state of Rio de Janeiro. Most days the temperature in the *subúrbios* is ten to fifteen degrees hotter than on the coast. The dry heat quickly evaporates the water in large rooftop storage containers so that the unreliable water pumps—built from scraps and ingenuity—need to run more frequently to transport water up to the rooftops from the pipes at street level, often breaking under the strain of this work. Today aridity and heat seem all the more unbearable because there is no water to pump. The pipes are empty. It is our third day without running water, and the reserve rooftop storage containers sit empty now too.

From my window I shout to Milene to wait for me as I see her and her daughter walking down the street. She is carrying two empty jerry cans, to transport water, in her hands. I rush down our stairs, grabbing two jugs of my own. We join a procession of women walking to the community's public *bico de agua* (water spigot), a pipe that juts up from the ground and then twists down so that people can fill a container from it. There is a black plastic faucet, and the water comes out of a neatly shorn bit of pipe. Women are walking back up the slight incline in the street with their water. I share a smile with the women I know, while Milene wears a grimace of determination and sends a happy *"bom dia, vai com Deus"* (good morning, go with God) to all who pass.

This morning the newspaper *O Dia* ran a news bulletin online, reporting that an electricity interruption at the Guandu Water Treatment Plant would "harm" water supply in central Rio and the Baixada Fluminense of Greater Rio, but water was expected to be back to normal in seventy-two hours. In the meantime residents of Rio were asked to avoid wasting the precious fluid. The bulletin seemed perfunctory, hardly five hundred words, buried amid more newsworthy stories. I telephoned multiple friends in wealthy city-center neighborhoods to ask if they too were experiencing a water shortage. No one was. Clearly, water had been diverted to the center, while harm had been sent in the direction of the *subúrbios*. The city had ensured no one in the elite areas of the city felt the impact.

During this water stoppage an intense odor began to emanate from the favelas in the western *subúrbios*. Without water to flush the self-built sewage systems, people's homes were ravaged by the odor of sitting feces and urine. In my time living in the *subúrbios,* this was no uncommon experience; water stoppages happened at least twice a year during the hottest months. Milene's disinfectant proved, of course, a ready remedy to this situation. With its mixture of floral perfume and the scent of bleachy cleanliness, people could reclaim and disinfect their spaces from the intrusion—manifest in its absence—of the state. If the state was backing up toilets, making people go without showers and preventing clothes from being washed, then God, in fragrant disinfectant form, made a different kind of sensorium possible.

Milene asks me inside her house to show me what Enzo, her husband, has brought home. Now three fifty-five-gallon tubs of fragrance are packed into the workshop. As she pries back the lid, an instantly jarring scent emerges, musky and acidic, and my eyes sting with tears. She implores me to stick my head inside the tub and take a deep breath. "Do you smell that?" she asks excitedly. Milene dips her homemade scoop into the fragrance and then slowly pours out a steady stream of it, so I can take in its scent. She smiles widely and sticks her own head into the blue tub. She resurfaces, laughing at the good fortune God has bestowed on them, saying, "It smells like a thousand angels marching, doesn't it?"

Milene asks me to pray and bottle with her. Her petite body fits nicely into this tiny workshop, adjacent to her kitchen. She can duck and turn and not bump into anything. She knows the room's angles, its corners, its limits. She knows how to move her body in this room she built from the ground up. She is hardened and firm, unrelenting in the gaze she casts on her children and neighbors. The heat of the morning is turning into the unbearable heat of the afternoon, but we continue mixing disinfectant before we break for lunch. We sit at the table and Milene pulls shut the curtain door to the kitchen. The children are home from school for lunch, and she relishes the opportunity to shoo them all from the kitchen so we can talk. As we eat, I pepper Milene with questions about the fragrance, wanting to ensure I have all the details right. But my questions seem to provoke an uncomfortable anxiety this afternoon. I ask her about the first time they took the fragrance, but Milene begins to cry: "Do you think we steal the fragrance?" She continues, not rhetorically, "Do you think that the fragrance doesn't come from God?" I am at a loss for an appropriate answer, and Milene seems shaken and unsure in a way I have never seen her. I tell her that I have never thought of it as theft, but that I have a hard time knowing whether it comes from God. Milene tells me that a woman came by recently to show her some dark-red marks resembling burns on a child's legs that had developed after the woman had scrubbed her sofa with the disinfectant. Similar burns often marked Milene and her children's skin after working with the fragrance. Did I think she was to blame for the children's sores too?

Milene's anxiety begins to channel into prayer. She pushes further, asking hard questions of me and herself: "Why do we take the fragrance at night then? Why do we take it in secret? Why hasn't Enzo simply asked for it?" And then, "If it burns us, why not others?" Her answer now takes the form of an Evangelical sermon. She poses the hard questions to the nonbeliever but is also slowly laying out pieces of God's puzzle, leading and urging me to nod along, to learn to see things in the same way as her so that, by the end of the sermon, we will have arrived together at a different outcome. She talks for a long time about this, circling around a number of uncertain scenarios: the company would certainly balk at their secondary use of the fragrance, she tells me. They think it is unsafe waste, and they barrel it up to dump it. Milene then counters herself, saying that they probably *could* ask for it. But, she warns, if the company could be convinced that it was not garbage, it would certainly demand payment—or worse, if Enzo asked a supervisor, then it was almost certain that the supervisor would try to extort him by making him pay a bribe. Milene acknowledges that she has seen many burns from the disinfectant, holding out her own hands as proof. But, she asks, isn't this why people like it? Don't they come for it *because* it burns away that which might do harm?

At this point she starts to preach about the dangers of being beholden to anyone but family and God. We talk out some more scenarios, but eventually Milene circles back to this gift and the scent itself: "The fragrance must be a gift from God," she says, "because God put the fragrance in our path. . . . I smelled it and I knew that we were saved. Smell it, and you will know. It smells like nothing else here," she says while gesturing around her. She finishes, "We belong to God, not to this place."

Milene tends carefully to her gifts from God. When new batches of fragrance arrive, she calls me excitedly on the phone. She always carefully pries back the barrel lids, allowing me to put my head right in, so I can appreciate a new scent and possibility. The actual fragrance and its accompanying scent matters.[5] Smell powerfully enables an affective and sensuous encounter with God. Here, as always, smell creeps into the spaces opened by emotional experience, personal memories, social history, and imagination. While telling me about her childhood, for example, Milene first conjures up its scent: the way the scent of seawater lay heavily across her life, working its way into her skin and hair to saturate every memory of the place. Here in this part of Rio, that scent of seawater is hard to come by. The valley that traps humidity produces an altogether different kind of air.[6] Smell, then, is at once connected to "transition," both temporal and material (Howes 1991, 128). Smell conjures the liminal, communicating to us something often invisible. Smell opens spaces that, as Anna Tsing writes, are at the same time both "present" and "ineffable" (2015, 37). Indeed, as Nicholas Shapiro notes, "smells are most pronounced at the crossing of thresholds" (2015, 374). For Milene and others who use divine disinfectant, these thresholds are multiple, material, sensed, and felt: center/suburban, Black/white, saved/sinner, cradled/abandoned.

The scent of grace is no small thing. Smell, morality, and Christianity have long been linked. Milene and other Evangelicals follow in a long line of Christians concerned with the medium of fragrance and the way odor can betray the existence of sanctity, while malodors can betray the existence of hell and immorality (Classen, Howes, and Synnott 1994). In *The Color of Angels*, Constance Classen explores the pre-Enlightenment idea of the odor of sanctity, or "the notion that Christians who lived in a state of grace would be infused with the divine scent of the Holy Spirit—the breath of God." Using perfumes to craft this kind of divinity, however, still inspired circumspection and anxiety. The early Christian Church considered perfumes a kind of "debauchery and idolatry," and even the role of divine fragrance—the trustworthiness of smell itself—was suspect (1998, 36, 44). Indeed, Classen describes a deodorized modernity's doubtfulness about smell more generally, with smell cast as an irrational sense compared to the supposed objectivity of sight. The distinction between Rio's center and its *subúrbios* is not sweet-smelling versus foul-smelling; rather, it is that the *subúrbios* dare to smell at all. To smell is to be premodern, even hellish.

Milene is clearly not without anxiety about where the waste fragrance originates, how it gets to her, and the harms and effects it might inflict on those it touches. As Matthew Engelke details, divine media can often cause apprehension about "whether a particular medium is a path to freedom or enslavement. Will this thing—this icon, this image, this book, this telephone, this computer—set me free or tie me down? Will it allow me to lead an authentic life (and in proper relation to the divine) or will it corrupt and cripple my ability to do so?" (2010, 377). As Milene's sermon shows, she also struggled with these questions. Could this waste product be multiple things: a God-given material from which to craft their future, a forgivable act of theft, *and* a potential for bodily harm? These are questions about the very possibility of grace in the city.

CONVERTING THE SUBURBS INTO SANCTUARIES

On a cool evening I attend an Evangelical service in the home of Janina, a neighbor of Milene's. At a midway break in the sermon, Janina emerges from her kitchen with a tray above her head, entering the large room at the front of her house. She begins to hand out small plates of stroganoff—a creamy chicken dish made from unsweetened condensed milk—for everyone seated in the room. The house smells of garlicky rice and the wet scent of canned palm hearts. The little plastic plates bend under the pressure of the generosity of this meal. We sit on a collection of mismatched chairs, collected from various spots over the years. Some people arrive with their own chairs, and others stand on the outer edges of the room or even lean in from the doorway and windows. Janina's husband passes out plastic cups, and we pass them around to one another, along with big bottles of cola and orange Fanta. We fill our cups and settle into our seats again, ready for more of the sermon. Once everyone has food, the preacher steps up to the microphone again, which is attached to a small sound system that Janina has rented for the evening. The sound system is not pointed at the group of us already here but faces the street. It carries the voice of the preacher into the evening heat. We eat and listen to this second round of preaching, and the congregants nod along between bites of food. Most of us here are close family and friends, with a few friends of friends in attendance too. The preacher is visiting from his own small church on the other side of town.

When we are finished eating, Janina's daughter collects our plates, and we rise to our feet again. The sound of the preacher's voice competes with a chorus of other preachers' voices that emerge from windows on nearby streets. It is 9:30 p.m., and Janina's home has been transformed into a small Evangelical church. Her home is not ornate or particularly large, and it has not been chosen as a spot to gather because it can hold many more people than any other house. Her house is a typical three-story building built by her family from the ground up on a small plot over the past two decades. Janina lives on the first floor with her husband and three children. On the second floor are her parents, and on the top floor are her sister, her sister's husband, and their young daughter. Like Milene and Enzo, they have pieced together their house over many years with materials bought, found, and scrapped together.

But Janina and her family haven't stopped building. Instead, like many Evangelical families, they are now slowly transforming the front rooms of their homes into small Evangelical churches, with open windows and doors that beckon to believers on the street. The work to do this is piece-meal, completed over many years as God reveals materials to them and through their hard work and dedication to the task. Building a sanctuary is a creative labor. They take down walls and doors and bars on windows, opening large spaces in homes; gather chairs, sofas, and materials for lecterns; and collect money to pay for a sound system, all to turn their own homes into homes for God and fellow believers.

In 2012 Janina and her family began the process of turning their front room into a public sanctuary by moving the kitchen from the front of their house to the back half of the house and cutting it in size. This was done so that the sanctuary would face the street. By 2016 they had expanded this sanctuary by laying a cement pad just outside their front stoop, creating an outdoor congregation space and thus claiming a large part of sidewalk and road space for God. At the first service they hosted at home in 2012, the only people in attendance were family and friends. But four years later it was a functioning public sanctuary that they had built themselves, with congregants who gathered from Batan and other nearby communities. Here the grace of God was not a *whoosh* or a scent; it was hard like cement. Grace was the feeling of hard pavement under your feet. The transformation of their house into a sanctuary was, Janina said, the kind of good works God desired of them. And she emphasized that it wasn't through *her* good work that she was saved. Rather, she had allowed herself to be worked through. Here, in cement, was proof that her salvation was an eternal promise. This homespun sanctuary was an *elaboration* of God's grace.

MAKING MARGINS DIVINE

In converting houses and sidewalks into sanctuaries, Janina and many others were also conditioning and producing the city space in specific ways. Various kinds of Christian materiality tend to be invoked colloquially when speaking about Catholicism but not, in the same ways, for Evangelicalism. Startling material apparitions appear in Catholicism: bleeding crucifixes, weeping statues of Mary, stigmata. This kind of materiality is rarely associated with Protestant Christianities, where the disavowal of a material presence of God is part and parcel of the Protestant Church's Reformation. In the Reformation Protestants' relationship with God became about immediacy—it no longer needed to be mediated by sacred objects or priests. Today Protestant Churches are often simple and not ornate. Their bareness and starkness reflect Protestants' bare and unadorned relationship with Jesus. I do not mean to stress that there are holdovers of Catholicism that echo in today's Evangelicalism in Brazil. Instead, I look at how the distinctive materiality I have so far described emerges from a constellation of conditions. In landscapes defined by abandonment, wasted materials have value, and that value is often attributed to God. In a place where the stakes of absence are so acute, a present God materializes in the form of valuable discards that can be pieced together into future-enabling forms. Here Evangelicals seem to focus on the mercy and unconditional nature of God's grace and the way that grace tends to appear in the margins. The margins are far from marginal; rather, they are generative spaces of potential.[7] Evangelicals in Rio's western *subúrbios* think a lot about the ways that God, through divine pieces of grace, enters homes and lives and enables a different conception of life or the city itself.[8]

In the *subúrbios* it seems we need to take seriously the way that the margins—and the scraps in the margins—become divine. These scraps as well as people's actual engagement with them through labor, smell, and touch, produce a visceral sensation of the divine working through their lives, dotting their paths with future possibilities. These scraps are actors that matter. Grace is sensed from the aroma of divine fragrance that goes right up the nose to the bars that slip through the hands, coming together to form a cart.

Chemical waste is made and discarded in the western *subúrbios*. It leaves the factory in a borrowed truck under the shelter of a blind eye. It is carefully crafted into a divine disinfectant in a piecemeal workshop next to a kitchen, then bottled in purchased trash from a trusted waste picker. Legs and a cart distribute it across a few communities, all with their own distinct forms of governance, and then sell it to local Evangelical home businesses. Sometime later Evangelicals who frequent those businesses take a bottle from the shelf. They use it lovingly to cultivate a scent and space of worth and security in a part of the city historically and currently constructed by systems of anti-Black practice.

A few bags of cement fall off the truck as it moves from one construction site to the next. It gets collected by a rubbish worker doing temporary contract work. He brings it home, and his family carefully crafts it into a home sanctuary, where people, dreams, and desires can collect in the evening. They share food and hopes and fears. The cement steadies their prayers, allowing them to reach out into the street, a street where the police roam, ready to curtail both life and joy.

I examine how this crafted optimism is tethered to histories and daily experiences of racial inequity and inequality both sensed and felt but also to a notion of a God who cradles above the fray without eclipsing the existence of the fray. Pieces of grace are a kind of mediation of the divine that makes new affective experiences possible. To make sense of this, however, requires also interrogating "the link between institutional power and interpretive practice," investigating how flows of power and empowerment, histories of harm and hope, come to haunt particular forms of mediation and their possible spaces: optimism alert to pessimism, wafting on the breeze, hard beneath your feet (Rutherford 2006, 106).

3 In Attention to Pain

"I have to hold it, like this," she says, clutching her lower abdomen under her shirt, in a stance that is both defensive (shoulders locked and angled) and embracing (her soft flesh cupped gently in her hand). Mara, a young Black woman recovering from an infected Cesarean incision—which has split open twice—shows me this pose before continuing her demonstration. We are inside the walled compound of a defunct motel, now home to multiple families and individuals. She shows me how she manages to open the heavy roadside gate between the motel and the highway while holding a baby car seat, in a way that does not further rupture her wound. Her twin daughters, born seven weeks premature and now two months old, are curled up together in the seat.

Mara has a trick for opening the heavy gate. She hoists the car seat into the air with her one free hand. Then, with a swift but careful toss, she bounces the car seat up in the air as she threads her arm through the handle to catch the seat on its descent. She does this while her other hand continues to hold her wound in place. The move jerks her body so violently that I gasp audibly and jump up to grab the carrier from her, making some of the others around us laugh. Mara smiles at her performance and my reaction and continues her story, her body enacting its details. She describes and shows how any time she leaves the motel compound she must

> put the babies down,
> push open the heavy gate,
> hold the gate open
> by jutting out my hip,
> hoist the car seat up
> using the method that made you gasp,
> edge myself along,
> lean forcefully against the metal,
> prevent it from swinging shut on its spring-coiled hinge,
> shuffle to the other side,
> then step quickly
> —almost a jump—
> so that it doesn't strike me sharply as I release,
> and it swings back shut.
>
> I'm out now.
> Thank God.
> Amen.

Mara bends to accommodate the gate, the walled compound, the sandy highway shoulder, and the streaming cars and trucks that whip sand into eyes. She accommodates the stares of men whose job it is to guard the gate but not to hold it open. Mara says that the Cesarean incision has split open twice doing these kinds of everyday tasks. Her body simmers, she says; it pulses in anticipation of pain when she makes the first move toward the gate, a slow bubbling. But when the wound rips, it boils. The pain boils over. All those moves, those tricks for moving her body, she says, are made to avoid that moment when the pain boils over. She masters tricks for bending *just* enough that the pressure doesn't break her, doesn't quite break her. She swallows the pain and bears it while still doing what must get done. It is a scheme for making her body bear the least amount of damage or pain, because no pain or damage is not an option here. When Mara finishes her explanation, we pray, then we talk, then we pray and talk again. We pray for bodies that can *bear* pain. Arms stretch to the sky, like hands reaching out for father and mother. I scribble a question in my field notes: "Where are the prayers for *no* pain?"

We sit together under a large tree next to the motel. The motel has been shuttered as a business for some time, and sunlight shines into the rooms through gaping holes in the exterior walls. The motel is almost swallowed up by noise from the grinding traffic that connects this small community to Rio's more famous downtown and beachside neighborhoods. Gaping holes aside, the building hums with life. It holds a collection of families with no other options. Mara sits with the other women, curled up in a circle of broken chairs and stools. The women happily make room for me here, keen to have me to sit and chat as our children play. My own daughter curls up in my lap for the few hours we sit together. She joins the other children in their games only once I pick up my things to leave, which causes me to stay even longer. She is teased for being shy: "She is not Brazilian," the women all quip. They question my mothering methods out loud, but they do so for most women, so I try not to let it bother me.

My first visits to this motel were mediated by community-health agents, a cadre of women and men from the community (or surrounding communities) who work in teams with a doctor and nurse from the local health clinic. We live around the corner, but, as Mara's description makes clear, it is complicated to move from the motel on the highway shoulder to the community of Batan. The health agents initially brought me to the motel in an attempt to shock me. They marched me to the top floor of the motel, where drug users converged. They loudly remarked how folks defecated openly here and prodded me for an appalled response. They forced a handkerchief to my face, trying to block my nose, talking loudly to me about the residents to shame them. I have since returned again and again without the health agents, now permitted to enter by the homegrown security guards who watch the gates. These are young men with guns, standing guard, often found chatting with the uniformed military police who will sometimes park their SUVs on the sandy shoulder outside the motel wall. Theirs is a fragile truce. They joke together until they are not joking anymore— one wrong move from the young men, and the uniformed officers will have them face down in the sand, guns pointed at the backs of their heads. I am allowed in because I first arrived with the health agents. It is clear that I am not *meaning* to harm (of course, that does not preclude unintentional or accidental harm).

TOUGHENING THROUGH PAIN

I pay attention to the distribution of pain, how bodily pain is experienced within certain landscapes, looking at the often trampled-over landscapes of Rio's *subúrbios*. In doing so I have tried to make explicit what has otherwise been implicit: the expectation in Rio's urban governance and racial capitalism that resilience means toughening through pain. Here poor, female, and Black residents are forced into arrangements of more painful lives than the privileged. City services, such as transportation and medical clinics, don't provide convenience only; they ameliorate pain. Pain, then, becomes unevenly distributed across the city through a mode of governance, capture, and distribution that produces and uses pain as a destructive anti-Black force. At the same time, Evangelicalism also works with bodily pain. Evangelicalism in Rio's suburbs is often caught up in this entanglement of pain, wounds, hopes, and desires, both cruel and optimistic. I turn to the ways by which Mara used Evangelical healing practices and ceremonies to link together pain and hope, demonstrating the importance of bodies and loving touch in this religious work and the care taken to produce and maintain hope under these conditions. As she performs rituals of love, touch, and prayer, lines of connection are laid down that form incipient community ties from which new relations of power begin and start their own process of accretion.

I consider how wounds matter—or not—in the *subúrbios* of Rio and how a wound's accompanying pain tells us something about how precarity can be felt, both bodily and affectively. The body and its wounds become ways to consider relations with the state and religion. This is part of the larger story of how in Rio, as elsewhere, bodies are always partly constituted through the practices and governance of racial capitalism and religious ordering, where Black women's bodies are made to bear the violence of white supremacy in the way it is enacted through space, policing, security, and labor, both physical and affective. In other words, bodily experience is shaped by anti-Blackness (J. Alves 2018) and gendered necropolitics (Caldwell 2007; Perry 2013; Smith 2016). Writing slowly, and using the deliberateness of that slow productive pace as a method to better attend to the plying and pushing forces that create bodies in pain,

I foreground, as Sara Ahmed explains, the ways that bodies are asked to "take more of it," bounce back, and never "snap" (2017, 189). While often forcibly bent and plied, bodily pain isn't always obvious. By slowing down I can sharpen the ethnographic focus to see not just the very literal bending and bouncing back that bodies do but also the damage this entails. I show how precariousness pains the body or, more precisely, how certain arrangements of precarity in Rio's suburbs hurt specific bodies in specific ways and how those bodies are made to bear that pain.

What does pain have to do with relations of power? Pain is not a universal; it is unevenly distributed. As Christen A. Smith explains, "the black body in pain" is part of the organization of Brazil: "Brazil's horizon of death erases the black body, not in the sense that it deletes it completely from existence, because it renders black people and black bodies as ghosts. . . . This is not to say that blackness can truly be reduced to this state of death and invisibility, but rather that this is the political project of state terror" (2016, 175; see also Mbembe 2001, 2017). Wounds function as everyday reminders of this terror. As Kia Caldwell notes, "[John] Burdick refers to the painful struggles faced by Afro-Brazilian women" in relation to citizenship and belonging "as 'the everyday wounds of color.' This phrase aptly describes the relentless personal torment that black women experience as a result of being judged according to anti-Black aesthetic standards. . . . Their experiences underscore the racialized and gendered significance of black women's bodies" (2003, 23).

PACIFICATION AND EXTRAORDINARY PAIN

I had originally come to the motel wanting to talk about pacification, a policing strategy that had been enforced in Batan a few years earlier. In 2009 Batan had been "pacified" after Rio's elite special-operation policing unit—Batalhão de Operações Policiais Especiais—had taken the favela back from a militia made up of off-duty police officers and firefighters. It was a huge story, making the *New York Times*. It made the news because of the story's sensationalism, involving undercover journalists, a kidnapping, and a militia. Batan, located in the western outskirts of the city, tens of miles away from the highly visible beachside favelas that usually attract so much attention, is used to being ignored. Pacification is often formally described as a combined policing, military, and urban-planning intervention premised on deposing nonstate armed groups and in the process reclaiming city space. It was meant to promote and extend the human rights of the poor residents of the city, folding these spaces back into the city under the wing of state security. Critically, Batan was the only community to be pacified that had once been controlled by a parastate militia (as opposed to a prison-based organized crime group). In some ways Batan had never really been separate from the enterprise of state-led security.

I asked about the day that the pacification force arrived. Viviane, a friend of Mara's, said that an armored personnel carrier, or a *caveirão* (big skull), drove into Batan's main square, along with military police officers riding on horseback, and dominated the community with a massive show of force. This is a story I'd heard before, both from Batan residents and other researchers. But, as Viviane finishes, another woman jumps in to disagree with her, saying that the *caveirão* was just a dream—a "vision," she calls it—"something concocted by the mind in order to mark time." Mara, nursing her twin girls, considers this. "Maybe this is true; maybe there was never a *caveirão*." Others give a noncommittal shrug about the looming *caveirão*. A few other women say they can't remember when pacification happened at all; this is strange, they think out loud, if its arrival was marked by a *caveirão* surrounded by horses. I ask the woman who called the *caveirão* a vision about a story someone else told me: on the day the police arrived, a helicopter buzzed overhead, releasing thousands of leaflets into the air announcing the community's "rescue." "That could have happened," she replies. And then she flips her story, saying, "and the *caveirão* could have happened too." Viviane then also changes her position, her voice lilting as she poses to the group of us, "Maybe the *caveirão* didn't happen?"[1]

Interspersed throughout this first conversation about pacification is Mara's account of coming to the motel. She explains that she was forced out of her small home by her then boyfriend (and father to her daughters). Her boyfriend thought the twins would be a hassle and a financial drain. Mara says she had trouble getting to the health clinic for her checkups while pregnant, and when she went into early labor, at just thirty-three weeks, the doctors were apathetic about the twins' developmental future.

Though the twins were born quite prematurely and required supple-
mental oxygen, they were discharged after just a week. To Mara this felt
woefully inadequate but also expected. She had pleaded with the hospital
that she had nowhere to go, no time to arrange housing, and no money.
The hospital—already overburdened and lacking beds—discharged her
anyway. She said this in itself was not surprising. She explained that her
time at the hospital had been marked by racist comments from nurses and
staff about her dark skin and her weight. She returned to her boyfriend's
apartment, but he wouldn't open the door. With few choices she carried
the twins together in the bucket-style car seat to the bus station and rode
to Batan with her small hospital bag; she arrived at the bus stop closest to
the motel, where a good friend lived. It was during the walk between the
bus stop and the motel that her brand new Cesarean incision ripped open
for the first time, bleeding though her shirt and pants. When Mara arrived
at the motel, her friend told her to go back to the local health clinic, a quar-
ter mile away. So she walked to the clinic, only to be loudly scolded by the
staff for her stupidity. Mara recalled how a nurse crudely joked about her
condition to another staff member while she restitched her.

Mara grew up in northeast Brazil, in a community in downtown São
Luís do Maranhão. She had come to Rio to be with the father of her twins
when she was just a teenager, moving to the western suburbs, at first not
permanently but just to try it out. She felt conflicted about returning now
to São Luís, not because her family would be unsupportive but because
she doubted there was a future there. In Rio, she said, you could at least
make some money. Maybe build a life, she said lightly. At the same time,
staying in the motel could be terrifying. On the third floor, she explained,
many people congregate to use drugs. Because of them, say the women
sitting with us, the police put armed guards at the gated motel entrance.
The police come by almost every night, with flashing lights and sirens.
They bang around the motel, shouting and shining flashlights into people's rooms, rooms that have curtains for doors. It wakes and frightens the
children. But Mara also worries that the pacification police will tire of
these nightly raids, and she wonders what this might mean for her safety.
One night she woke to find a half-naked man in her room trying to light
the stove. When they tried to get him out of the room, he grabbed a knife
from the counter and began to wave it wildly at them. Mara found herself

contemplating each night whether she would be better off with the police hanging around the motel or without them. We prayed again, Mara leading the group in prayer. This time we prayed for safe sleep, for safe rest. The conversations move like this, in and out of prayer.

Amid this backdrop of pacification, Mara struggles to get her twin daughters the kind of health care and watchful eye that she believes they need. When she arrives at the clinic for treatment, either for herself or the twins, the nurses always comment on her weight. Mara is Black, and her figure is heavy. She says that the nurses laughed out loud at her for this. With pacification came a brand new Clínica da Família (Family Health Clinic) on the edge of Batan, serving both Batan and the surrounding Realengo region. But the new health center was typical of the absence and presence of the state. It was freshly painted white and blue, with large grounds, a seniors' exercise center, and long rows of offices, with plenty of seating inside. What it lacked, of course, was doctors. It was an empty container with a crisp paint job. Critical services were also lacking—staff were not trained to draw blood, so anything that involved a blood test required a referral to a nearby and equally understaffed and underequipped hospital.

Bodies bend to accommodate these rhythms of absence and presence, crude laughter, swinging hard gates, the desire and ambivalence for police. Mara's story encapsulates struggles against abandonment. The practices of abandonment work like a litany of painful pecks—the slights, the wounds, the indignities that add up. Such descriptions have been well developed by scholars of Brazil, who have detailed the very particular conditions here—specifically, the ways precarity often hinges on, and is enforced by, the violent binary between the *morro* (hill) and *asfalto* (pavement). Ben Penglase, for example, vividly depicts the very material—and at the same time spectral—anxieties about "stray bullets" (2011, 412). He writes that daily life in Rio's favelas is governed by "everyday emergencies" (2009, 47), a concept that considers the ways insecurity upends but also organizes normalcy, something akin to uncertainty being the only certainty in these spaces. João Biehl (2005), working from Orlando Patterson's (1982) concept of social death, ties the experiences of precariousness and abandonment to the concepts of social death and the disposability of Blackness, where abandonment functions as an ongoing relation of governance, working on and through bodies, dehumanizing them but not killing them outright. For Mara the toll of the public-health nurses' jabs and the little pecks at her body and worth added to the daily indignities that piled up over the years. She cataloged these harms as bodily pains in a landscape intent on harming her. The toll this took could be heard in her sighs, as her body cramped inward while she carefully recounted her day to me, ticking off the feats of endurance—like opening a gate—that she had practiced this day, this week, this month, this decade.

These narratives about pacification were interwoven with an account of the pain and the work required to open a gate. This was not happenstance. The story of pacification in Batan was itself a story of extraordinary bodily pain, but a certain kind of pain, experienced by certain kinds of people. Elizabeth Povinelli describes how governance by abandonment happens as "quasi-events [that] never quite achieve the status of having occurred or taken place. They neither happen nor not happen," such that mundane kinds of violence are rarely aggregated or understood. This is unlike "events" that entail an "ethical demand." These "seem to necessitate ethical reflection and political and civic engagement" (2011, 13–14).[2] For many residents of Batan, the torture of the journalists by the militia, with intersections of privilege, race, and class, was understood to necessitate an ethical response from the state. Pacification figured as the ethical response to the journalists' torture, not as a response to the structural obstacles and pain that they experience every day. For residents this selective attention to their community lays bare the ways that the promises of pacification were never sincere. Selective attention operates with purpose; it is a tool of anti-Blackness in the city, which renders a notion of abandonment often too diffuse to pin down. Selective attention—from the state, the media, the police—taunts and jeers: How can people claim we don't care if we have given them a pacification force? In 2018 the pacification force was removed from Batan. In the end pacification certainly was—as these women explained in various modes—a fleeting and undependable process.

EVANGELICALISM AND HEALING TOUCH

Mara pulls down the elastic top of her tank top to nurse one of the twins. She slides her breast out, and the tight elastic of her shirt cuts into her skin.

Her girlfriend, Claudia, joins the circle and rubs lotion through Mara's hair, neck, shoulder, and lower back. The lotion smells good—of sweet fruits, a bit too strong, but also just right. Claudia's fingers press into Mara's skin, leaving delicate fingertip marks, as she lovingly spreads the lotion. In response the skin shimmers. Mara straightens at times when Claudia pushes too hard; otherwise, she relaxes. It is intimate and kind, and one of the women sitting next to her says, "Okay, me now!" Claudia shifts slightly, turning around, and begins to massage the lotion into the other woman's hair. Mara takes this moment to turn to me and describe how her boyfriend used to beat her: he would punch and kick until she would crumple to the floor or against the wall. *Bang. Bang. Bang.* She remembers that the floor was always cold, the punches always hot, each punch a burn, often so hard she would pass out. The women laugh at the story, at men in general, cursing them through chuckles. Mara takes her infant off her breast and leads us in prayer again. She grips my hand and lifts it to the sky. With our fingers interlinked, I also become slippery with lotion. This time it is a hollering prayer. It turns the heads of the boys and men who stand guard at the door. She prays for strength for each of us in the circle.

I have often come to this abandoned motel-turned–temporary housing, only to find that the person I was there to see wasn't there anymore. I held Mara's hand tighter. People move on from this space. It's not a place of nostalgia and fond memories. Best to keep on moving, as the police pass and glare through the gate. The prayer moves our bodies, and I look up to the sky and its extravagance. I try to firmly plant myself on this shifting ground. As I write this, I can remember the scent of the lotion. These words nudge the part of my brain where smells are both hidden and found.

Later that same month, in a prayer and healing circle, Mara lifts her shirt to reveal her wound as we close ranks around her body. She lies on her bed and the preacher raises her voice, calling on God to heal her. It is both a general and a specific request. The woman preacher, with her curly hair bouncing as she commands the small motel room, rocking on her toes, asks God to ensure that this is the last round of stitches. She asks for the stitches on Mara's Cesarean wound to hold, for God to heal Mara's body, and for her to be relieved of this pain. She tells God that Mara has endured her pain well, like a faithful servant, and that she has been tough and strong and cheerful and dutiful to God's will. But she asks for this to be finished now, for the pain to cease, for the wound to close, for Mara to be made whole. Our bodies fold over Mara as we lean over her bed. We pulse together, willing her body, this room, this motel, to suture and heal her. We've lit the room with candles, but the holes in the exterior wall let in light from cars on the highway as they whiz past. A lamp rigged in the hall illuminates the red sheet used as a door; when people walk by, they appear to be shadows.

"Are we in the motel anymore?" I wonder in my field notes. There is an effort to transport, to render the prayer circle itself as a real space and place in which we can reside, momentarily at least. This is a space and place constituted through prayer. In this motel room, huddled together in prayer over Mara's wounded body, the preacher gently asks us to lay our hands on her. Our hands, soaked with sweat, touch her body. Our fingers have traced babies faces, interlocked with loved ones, tickled backs, scrubbed floors, prepped lunches, written letters, split open oranges. We tighten these fingers around her legs and arms. We clench our fingers around her and hold tight while the preacher prays. The prayer circle reverberates, and, as we rest healing hands, we are transported. In that moment the broken walls of the motel fall away. They crumble into a dust that turns into a starry night sky that guides our way to an otherwise constellation of life. The preacher says, "Hold hands now. We are leaving. We are going to God . . . to dignity. . . . In the hands of Jesus, she will be saved."

An optimism takes root here in this space. It is not an insensible hope based on a naive understanding of God. It is an optimism that is alert to pain and violence but takes care to cultivate hope regardless. Certainly, the forms of care that Evangelicalism offers can also be spiny and punitive. White supremacy, for example, cultivated through much Evangelical ordering in Rio, is invented and justified through religious practices. Like all forms of white supremacy, it is often both violent and "cultivated lovingly" through spacialized whiteness and anti-Blackness, exclusion, and cunning convenience (White 2018). Yet hopeful futures can still emerge from this prickly tethering to pain and its harms. There are friendships, shared food, and invitations to join. Bodies together in this room alternate between laughter, tears, and prayer but also violence, lost children, hard labor, forced sex, and even more that is mundane—bending the body one way and then another, demanding that it does not break.

This tethering often happens through touch—as our bodies touch, as we give ourselves over to the affection of the group. Putting our hands on Mara, we attempt to cultivate something different than the violence that has brought us together here. This is not just a group of neighbors; for a few brief seconds, we are a body joined, pulsing, loving, and striving to feel God's presence. At this moment healing touch is a kind of shelter in its own right, a shared and felt experience of belonging and respite. Loving touch is central to this experience, women explained to me, a counterweight to violence. Touch is "effectual," writes Eve Sedgwick, who notes that touch "makes nonsense out of any dualistic understanding of agency and passivity" (2003, 14). Bodies respond to touch. This night in the motel room, the touch of the prayer circle for Mara is magnetic: it gathers bits of good feeling and pleasure together so that they multiply and are shared among us. This closeness is cultivated, forged through religious touch and invitation. It is a productive force that creates community ties that themselves can begin to accrue strength and power. Sensory encounters are relational encounters that always exceed the body but are nonetheless tethered to the body's very materialities and oppressions.

ORGANIZING ATTENTION

Pain in the body can organize attention, prayer, a sermon, and the city, in much the same way that attention itself organizes pain. We see this by where pain is permitted to happen and where it is not, where pain is attended to and where it is not. To bear pain is itself a kind of prayer, because Evangelicals are meant to give their pain over to God and in return to be relieved of it. Believers I worked with explained that to bear pain, to weather it with a faith that one day they would be relieved, is a way to experience God's grace. This grace can sometimes appear in a healing ceremony, but many suggested they were okay with striking a lifetime bargain: pain on Earth for eternal salvation. In this way pain and its emotional, psychological, and physical attributes are tied to the possibility of change. Pain and hope are tethered to each other. In the present life one doesn't exist without the other. They are mutually constitutive. To have hopes of heaven is to know deep—and often mundane—pain. To pray is to pay attention to and care for that pain, to care for others around you, and to turn pain into love and possibility.

During my fieldwork I saw this most often through these intimate prayer encounters, specifically the use of healing touch as a way to constitute new kinds of care and love for bodies and lives. As Marleen de Witte notes, writing on charismatic Pentecostalism in Ghana, we can think about "touch as an entry point to the question of the relationship between body and spirit" (2011, 493–94). In Latin America scholars of Evangelicalism have argued that Evangelicalism somehow empowers or provides security amid the changes wrought by modernity and capitalism. Evangelicalism is at times conceptualized as a kind of protective community that families can join to shield themselves from gang- and drug-related violence. The use of healing touch as a method to secure makes sense here, albeit somehow differently than as previously described. Hands are often laid on bodies while praying as an aid to the flow of the Holy Spirit to secure it against harm, as a form of loving protection, and as a mode of communicating worth. I was often instructed by pastors and believers to let my body be a channel for the flow of the Holy Spirit. Bodies of friends, loved ones, pastors, and neighbors, both surrounding and touching the wounded in prayer, are part of the transition from injury to healing, part of constituting a distinct community that centers the injured as worthy of attention. Attention *and* inattention both organize and delimit. The tactility of the Holy Spirit, felt through the laying of gentle hands on the body of the wounded, is something of a counterweight to the ongoing and lived experiences of the presence and absence of the state. The pain-making state is not gentle here.

A few weeks after the healing ceremony, Mara's wound opened again. The infection was persistent, and in the end it took many months and consistent treatment in a nearby hospital for her to fully recover. This was alongside consistent prayer and healing touch. A method of slow attention and slow writing allows research to be attuned to this "alongside" or beside. As Sedgwick writes, "Beside is an interesting proposition . . . because there's nothing very dualistic about it. . . . Beside permits a spacious agnosticism about several of the linear logics that enforce dualistic thinking" (2003, 8). "Beside" is a way to think seriously about not just how bodies are governed but also how bodies perceive, mold, bend, slack, and reverberate. The body is not just a prison, governable and governing. It alights. An attention to this requires attention to how bodies both constitute and perceive. In doing so I am working through a theory of power that foregrounds the senses, feeling, and emotion, to better understand the force and work of religious communities and the lived experience of precarity and abandonment. Evangelical faith—as one potential beside—lets me pay attention as it swells into being, while still leaning on, warping from, and touching dominant modes but without necessarily being insurgent—or linear—in construction. Indeed, thinking our way beside is a "project of thinking otherwise" (11). In other words, the way out of spaces where power is defined by prohibition, repression, and discipline cannot be through the counterpoints of liberation or insurgence but instead through the growth of occupying an "other"—or at least a "beside."

SHIFTING ATTENTION

State and religious institutions form a productive as well as a repressive matrix of space and time through which bodies and selves emerge; both operate—at least partly—through particular uses of injury and pain. As Robert Samet writes of Venezuelan populist politics, "the material experience of injury" organizes political subjectivity through "affective force" (2019, 274). Mara, enduring multiple forms of direct violence and inattention to her pain from the state, goes on to abide in and create a community of hope and love, also through an attention to pain and suffering through intimate healing touch. This matters because these *subúrbios*, like Brazil more broadly, is riven by the inequalities created by cruel structural hierarchies. There is a hierarchy of gender and color, as Mara's femaleness and Blackness are used to categorize and castigate her. There is the hierarchy of service provision, as a new but nearly empty clinic is built to serve these *suúrbios*, while highways speed motorists through the *suúrbios* like they are nowhere worth stopping or knowing. There is a hierarchy of attention that determines which modes of response are possible or even ever permitted.

Moving slowly through bodily pain, Evangelical touch, and the various uses of bodily sensation—and the emotions that accompany them—offers another way to think through this politics of attention in Rio's *subúrbios* and the vicissitudes of anti-Blackness on Rio's flatlands. Amid these long-standing structural questions of racial violence in Brazil, the absence and presence of state governance by omission, and the depoliticization of capitalism, Evangelicalism has emerged as a distinctive mode that has enabled many people to turn their attention away from a politics of making demands on the state and toward a politics of salvation, a felt politics of worth that lies both in and beyond the landscapes of the *subúrbios*. An attention to attention matters, then, as attention is an ethnographic mode, technique of governance, and form of refusal (Simpson 2014). Attention can bring what matters into relief. Practices that shift attention—like a healing ceremony in a crumbling motel—open new ways of thinking through precarity, care, and subjectivity. Pain throws into relief how bodies are never just mere vessels of the self, beings to be impinged on by governing forces, but alight as intimate projects of connection and power.

Over the past decade ethnographies of bodies that move, perceive, and react—bodies that bristle, simmer, deflate, and pulse—have become entry points to understanding the emotionally charged and sensorially rich ways that worlds are generated and endured. These modes of ethnographic attention have allowed anthropologists to attend to bodily sensation and affect as it actually exists—that is, in conversation with power relations. Attending to quotidian bodily and sensory experience illuminates what is political about them.[3] I think of this as similar to how Thomas Csordas notes that to "attend to a bodily sensation is not to attend to the body as an isolated object, but to attend to the body's situation in the world" (1993, 138). But, in addition, to each of us, sensation is the world.

Erica Caple James takes this up, advancing Csdoras's theory of the body in the world, and the world in the body. Her ethnography of (in)security and pain in Haiti, informed by her work as a practitioner of the Trager method of "movement education," helped guide my own attention to the role of touch in forming and maintaining embodied relations. Slow attention allowed me to use touch as a research method and an avenue of understanding. James writes, "Through the interview process, I began to understand my clients' embodied self-awareness and the way they experienced their 'situation in the world.' The physical work with my clients added another dimension in which the somatic mode of attention was communicated and perceived through *touch.*" Touch, James explains, can be used as a "primary vehicle of communication" (2010, 147, 148; emphasis added). As James develops it, a more material approach to the anthropology of the body depends on advancing a generous ethnographic sensibility that goes beyond careful listening and observing.

This more capacious and slow approach ties together the politics of bodily experience and feeling with an analysis of how bodies are made through racial, spatial, and colonial governance over landscapes. Thus, this work both grapples with and extends previous work in Brazil that investigates bodies as they exist in and through power relations (Caldwell 2007; Edmonds 2010; Smith 2016; J. Alves 2018). Ugo Felicia Edu argues, "Recognition and interrogation of the aesthetic underpinnings of health and biomedical systems will facilitate disrupting how these same systems contribute to the construction and perpetuation of notions of blackness and whiteness, and their relationships to disease, ugliness, death, health, beauty and life" (2019, 681).

Pain is an acute way to think this through. In its multitude of forms, pain is a lived-in condition for many who make their lives in Rio's suburbs. And simmering pain—that which can boil up and then return to simmering, as Mara experiences—is an especially pertinent way of describing many concurrent issues related to (in)security, anti-Blackness, violence, poverty, and inequitable access to infrastructures, such as hospitals, electricity, and water supplies. At the same time, these communities are often "pains" to the city, spaces that authorities would like to see "cleaned up" or made to disappear from view. Rio's *subúrbios* are places where pain is displaced, where a laborer's pained feet are finally allowed to be seen or where painful substances—like the asbestos and chemical plants, for example— can be set up or where a prison can be built to hold and make pain.

Rio's suburbs are often used as containers of pain, constructed and used to keep it apart from the Marvelous City. As Keisha-Khan Y. Perry writes, "Spatial exclusion is at the core of gendered racial stratification in Brazilian cities" (2013, xv). Pain may be spatially displaced or made invisible, but it still remains in the sensorial and affective registers. To decenter pain to the suburbs creates an "invisible geography" that can more conveniently be denied (Scarry 1985, 3). Smith writes of "the Black body in pain" as the very foundation of Brazil's choreography and its counterpart to the scripted performance of "Afro-paradise." The economies of paradise are really "economies of Black suffering" (2016, 175). Smith reminds us how pain organizes experience: "Invented cultural ideas, thoughts, and values become concrete in our minds when we associate them with the incontrovertible truth of the body in pain. Things that are intangible, fluid, nebulous, or otherwise difficult to grasp become experienceable when we can conceive of them in the material terms of the body" (65). Wounds—physical, material, and social—can tell us about how pain organizes and delimits bodies, cities, and worlds. Evangelical healing here, always coupled to the wound itself, can tell us about how love, touch, and prayer might be kinds of scar tissue, stitching together injuries and repairing the body as a site of hope and connection.

4 Wolves at the Heels

Vandila's sweaty palm grips mine as we stand shoulder to shoulder in a tight prayer circle in her home. I can feel the bristle of her goose bumps against my skin as her arm presses into mine. Our bodies seem momentarily joined, as we breathe as one, speak as one, and endeavor to hear as one. My large pregnant belly juts out into the center of our circle, and some people reach out to lay a hand on it as well. As each of us take our turn to pray, Vandila prays for the children around us. Their movement is compelling. They flutter and flit, cry out and laugh, like the group of dancing and uncontainable angels in our midst. The angels, Vandila preaches, will move among us. Someone says they bounce through us, having fun with one another. They tempt us with their joy, as they help us push back against the demons who clutter the room too, trying to hold tight to bodies, pestering the skin, like boils. Vandila swats them away through prayer, casting them out. Later she tells me that the demons skulk in the shadows, purring at us to let them back in, mewing like cats that need tending. They cleave to us, not liking when we try to release ourselves from them. They whine in the corner, waiting until we are weak again and willing to feed them. The baby in my belly somersaults, and the group squeals with joy at the strange bulges that push up against my skin toward their hands.

Another child bounces through the middle of our pulsing—squeezing between legs to find, then cling to, the leg of her mother. The circle opens and closes as more people come up the stairs to join in, drawn by the music and bright lights from the open window. Home from work and errands, they find themselves pulled in by voices united in prayer. As they enter, they are grasped and held firm. They are made part of the circle.

Vandila exhales audibly when her husband and son enter the room and join the prayer circle. She pitches her body toward them in embrace, pulling them into the circle, gripping them tightly, wrapping others' arms around them. We expand and contract. We do not deflate; we float. Our circle widens, enveloping the newcomers, creating new corners. Buoying in the night air, we are a house on fire, flames taking in everything, joining us together through captivating fumes that will not leave anyone alone for long. The prayer circle does not break, even with the demons lapping at our heels. The angels hold us firm, together.

Tonight no one speaks in tongues or feels the Holy Spirit directly move within their body. In fact, this rarely occurs on nights like these. Instead, something joyful is made while praising God, a stretched moment of touch, intimacy, and feeling that—even if not explicitly—produces an encounter with God that shakes our bodies and leaves women and men feeling full rather than empty. After a long day's work, it feels good to grasp the hand of someone next to you, to lean on them, and to raise up your voice to the heavens. As the circle breaks up, we wipe the sweat from our brows and collapse into chairs scattered throughout the room. Vandila brings out a cake from the kitchen. She slices it into neat squares, placing each one on a napkin, and hands them out to us. We hold out our plastic cups for another round of soda, doled out by her son.

At 9:00 p.m. this intimate prayer circle seems to have started the day afresh. Everyone looks more relaxed than they did an hour ago, when they had just arrived from work. They slump happily into sofas, digging into the well-earned cake. Life feels good and pleasurable from this vantage of renewal and the joy of being together. This circle—crammed with neighbors, family, angels, and God's presence—has opened a space where pleasure is both possible and considerable. Vandila sits on her husband's lap now, their bodies intertwined as they kiss and whisper. But renewal is also about fear, fear that this good connection cannot be sustained. Some people return to one another to rekindle it, often night after night. In this search for joy and intimacy, there is also fear that families will be ripped apart, that someone might not make it home, that another child will be lost. This is a fear rooted in a historical and present violence that has, without exception, ravaged each person in tonight's circle, a violence that reverberates in their families and their communities often at the hands of the state.

Earlier that morning I sat with Vandila while she scolded her teenage son: "You do not hit the wolf and then ask that he not eat you," Vandila explained to him, as she scraped the cuticles of her neighbor's fingernails. I sat in the front room of Vandila's house—which she had turned into a small manicure and pedicure salon—amid hundreds of name-brand polish bottles that she'd purchased secondhand at a discounted price because they were nearly empty. Vandila sat on a small stool as she chastised her son. He was thinking about attending a protest in the center of the city, and Vandila was steadfastly against it. The protests, ostensibly about a proposed hike in bus fares, were led by the Movimento Passe Livre (Free Pass Movement), which aimed to make public transit free to all in the city. But the protests had escalated across Brazilian cities, and Movimento Passe Livre became a rallying cry for better access, not just to public transit but also to public health, education, and public spending. The protests were highlighting the plight of poor urban dwellers and the mismanagement of public funds in the lead-up to the 2014 World Cup and 2016 Olympics. While students initially led the protests, the radio blared about the movement growing, about the "urban poor" and the "new middle classes" taking to the streets. The streets were full of people every night, and activists and academics were highlighting these protests as a momentous shift in how these urban poor would allow themselves to be treated.

But the Evangelicals whom I lived and worked with were not taking to the streets. To them taking to the streets was a unilaterally dangerous and useless act, especially for people like themselves—that is, Black and poor. Protests, Vandila said, were an exhausted route. Vandila advised her son to go to church rather than the protest, which is what he did that night instead, later posting photos to his Facebook feed of the uplifting service. Both his and her Blackness shape her notion of protest. Racism and white supremacy underwrite a reticence and realism to the potential of protest and the kinds of justice a citizen might feel entitled to. For those in the *subúrbios,* it is often true that injustice is all encompassing, which makes it more reasonable to follow an alternative course and sidestep out of the gaze of the state. Vandila told her Black son to not protest and deterred him from taking to the streets, advice rooted in experience with a system where his (likely) death would be as unexceptional as the poverty in which he was raised.

Vandila grew up in the *subúrbios* in a community controlled by traffickers; she once described that experience as a kind of ongoing panic. Her childhood, she explained, was marked by the traffickers' violence: Vandila lived in one of the tallest houses in her community, and her own bedroom window looked out over a neighboring community. During the frequent nighttime shoot-outs between trafficking groups, the traffickers in her community would enter her home to set up their firing stations from her top-floor bedroom as she tried to sleep. She would awaken each night to the sounds of gunfire and men drinking. She explained, "Nobody could stop them from coming in, and my father couldn't even come into my room while this was happening. I would lie there with my eyes closed, just pretending to sleep, hoping that they would not hurt me."

A few days after the protest that her son did not attend, we learned of the comments of a well-known former military-police captain on a popular newscast: unironically noting the outsider status of Rio's favelas, he suggested that the use of rifles to quell the protestors in downtown Rio was dangerous, arguing that "rifles should be used in war . . . in police operations in the communities and *favelas.* It is not a weapon to be used in an urban area" (Sousa Silva 2013; emphasis added). Here the captain casts the favela as a war zone, somehow distinct from the urban. I turned to Vandila and asked her to explain to me—yet again—how she could have hope in such a context: How can something as intangible as faith counter this seeming madness of the state? What can a prayer circle offer that might counter that? The captain's words obliterated her home and community as well as the joy found there. He wanted to deny them that possibility. Vandila simply answered by describing the image of Jesus hanging on the cross. She described how Pontius Pilate turned to the weakened and fragile son of God, saying, "Behold this man"; it was a crass joke that bedeviled his once-mighty presence. That image of Jesus on the cross—tormented and fragile but destined to live again—was the image she conjured for me as an answer. Pontius was wrong, she offered. "He carried out his violence, but he was wrong. The truth was right in front of him, but he couldn't see. But his denial didn't matter." The spectacular violence rendered against the favela and the people who live there is a crass joke, a threat, and a form of denial of everything they are. Softened now, rather empty after that description, she parsed Psalm 55 for me: "When you have a burden, give it to Jesus. The righteous cannot be shaken." Faith is not a counterpoint but a wholly different conception of life and its worth. Their worth will not be shaken.

The joy found and made in the prayer circle cannot be made small and insignificant. If anything, Vandila was daring to compare the joyfulness there in the circle to the might of military action in a war zone. Both are kinds and varieties of strength and power. Here I consider the prayer circle (and experiences like it) as a form of graceful refusal, where the prayer circle is also an arc of refusing the state and its so-called gifts of security, promise, and potential. It refuses through the production and giving of joy, tenderness, and grace. Refusal is not disengagement but a way of imagining through the construction of new terms and possibilities. The children running among us, the hands held tight, the prayers swinging through the air—the prayer circle can be engaged as a kind of space making that is not a recognition but a way to seek future elsewhere.

A growing body of work in anthropology dubbed the "anthropology of the good" (Robbins 2013) pays attention to how aspiration and striving matter (Rogers 2009, 32). An attention to this purported good is important and an ongoing contention of mine throughout the manuscript. But understanding the good in Rio's western *subúrbios* requires attention to the material impact of racism and anti-Black order and the ways that they both construct and govern the good itself. To think about the good under conditions of racism and oppression, I turn to critical race theory (Sexton 2011; Drabinski 2015; Sharpe 2016). John Drabinski (2015), for example, queries the place of affective optimism inside pessimism and abjection, and here I follow suit. As Drabinski notes, "The vicissitudes of affect under regimes of anti-Black racism" are tied "not just to forms of resistance amidst the pessimist's story, but also to how forms of life live alongside, against, or even wholly outside the sorts of abjection" imposed on Black life (and death). To view the prayer circle as a graceful refusal means opening the possibility of an existence of an otherwise (Crawley 2017) or perhaps a fugitivity (Sojoyner 2017) from the *subúrbios* as they are made and constructed and acted on by the state. The prayer circle is joyful refusal: haunted and burdened by past and present violence but brimming with a sense of the possible—of what will come. Fingers interlace, refusing to break, a pulsing joy in the circle.

REJECTING THE BOLSA FAMÍLIA

I was sitting with Ana and Milene on their front stoop one afternoon. It was about five o'clock. This was the time of day that everyone would start coming outside, to sit together as the weather began to cool. The kids would play in the street and on the front porch, running up and down the stairs together and between our small apartments. We were chatting about their disinfectant business, and I brought up the Bolsa Família, the much-acclaimed conditional cash-transfer program in Brazil.[1] To my surprise Milene explained that both she and Ana wouldn't accept it:

> I have the two boys here that I am fostering from the [Evangelical] Church—I don't have their identity or birth documents. Their mother went to the church and said she couldn't take care of them because she needed to go back to the north [of Brazil], and then the church asked me to take them in, so I did. And Denise, she is my adopted daughter, but I don't have her documents. But she's been with me since she was just a baby. If I took the *bolsa,* I would need to let the [community-health] agent into the house, and I don't have the children's documents to show her. But God brought them to me, and my work is to care for them. This is where they are meant to stay. The government is dangerous, right? They might take the children? It isn't safe to take the *bolsa.* We have God, and God provides, we don't need more.

This response was surprising, because both Milene and Ana could be seen as typical candidates to receive the *bolsa.* Ana was a single mother, raising her daughter on her own, while living with her brother and sister-in-law and their families. Their combined household income, in 2012, supporting twelve people, including seven children under fifteen and one child under eighteen, was approximately R$1,000 in a good month.[2] Depending on the time of year, eleven to thirteen members of the family lived together, including the two young boys they were fostering. Their income was large compared to many families, however, as Enzo had a job in a local factory, making approximately R$900 per month. The last R$100 each month was variable, as it came from Ana and Milene's various informal work activities, including the sweets and drinks cart that Ana runs and the disinfectant business.

Milene's description of the state as "dangerous" and the *bolsa* as an unsafe option expresses a concern voiced to me by many other Evangelicals in Rio's western *subúrbios*. They did not want to be made visible to the state, as being seen might actually further endanger them under a particular form of care that they saw as a potential imposition and threat. This kind of concern was voiced across a spectrum of issues, from not reporting incidences of gender-based violence because of a mistrust of police to not seeking medical care because the public-health system was understood to be saturated with race-based violence. For Milene and many more women and men like her, when a health agent entered their home it was a moment of apprehension and uncertainty, a moment when they felt the state had them in their sights. They never knew if it was the beneficent or malevolent version of the state knocking at their door.

"You never know what they will demand to see," Milene continued. Community-health agents are women and men from the community or surrounding community who work in teams with a doctor and nurse. When they register a family, they fill out an extensive form with the full names, dates of birth, and vaccination records of all people in a household, including identity and registration documents. The health agents, then, are the front lines of public-health bureaucracy. They knock on doors— and enter homes—to ensure that people see a doctor when they need to. They may also arrange for a doctor to visit homes if people are unable to travel to the health clinic. Over the course of my time in Brazil, I have often worked directly with community-health agents, as they operate as locally knowledgeable go-betweens for community members and underfunded and understaffed local health clinics. Community-health agents know people—their lives and histories. They are often privy to community gossip about family life, work, and even drug use or violence. They know when to call in extra help and medical assistance for people struggling with various health issues or what family to contact if someone is in need.

In general, they tend to know things about people—that is, the kind of things that people are uncomfortable (or downright fearful) of the state knowing.[3]

In this way community-health workers have become for many people something akin to the edge of the state—a rough spot that people have to maneuver while they seek care in underfunded systems that rarely account for structural harms. And the health agents are, of course, subject to much discussion and gossip about their intrusions. They are a central component of the actual materiality of the state in people's lives. The state is certainly not a continuous entity—it is stitched together through bits of material and nonmaterial presence and absence, but it is often felt by Evangelicals like a continuous and suffocating mass that they attempt to duck and dodge. For many even the seemingly mundane practice of having a community-health agent enter their home and document their family can feel anything but mundane. Rather, they become interpreted as further proof of the state's reach and its potential for violence and intrusion.

This, of course, extends beyond the *bolsa* or community-health agents. For example, rather than reporting gender-based violence to police, children and mothers—sometimes together and sometimes separately—often move between Rio de Janeiro and their home communities in Brazil's northeast as a form of response and support. For many migrant families, even if they had been in Rio for a decade or more, their networks of dependable family and friends are all located thousands of miles away. This happened time and again during my research: whenever there is a substantive family crisis—a death, an illness or injury, an arrest, or a dispute between spouses—people would move between Rio and their original northeastern homes. Simply put, the people they could lean on are on the other side of the country. Whenever that extra cushion of support is needed, someone would travel the approximately 1,800 miles between Rio and their hometown on an expensive multiday bus trip.

Parts of families are almost always on the move. Children, then, are moved between houses for informal fostering for short periods (a few weeks) or long periods (a few years) while moves are made permanent by finding work or sorting out a domestic conflict. Evangelical churches have become a fulcrum for this kind of informal fostering, often arranging the movement of children between families while biological parents sort out their living situations between Rio and the northeast. Milene was fostering two young boys—five and seven—while their mother returned to São Luís after violence between her and the boys' father erupted to unmanageable and unpredictable levels. The woman had gone to her Evangelical pastor for support, and he had advised her to leave the children with someone he trusted—Milene—while she returned to São Luís to be with her family and allow time to "heal her marriage." This woman had fled the house she shared with her husband, arrived on Milene's doorstep one evening with the boys and the pastor's instructions, and Milene took them in, not knowing for how long they would be in her care. The boys' mother did not have any of their documents; she brought with her only a small bag of clothes. That was not what was important. What was important was that she could trust Milene.

For Milene engaging with a health agent or seeking out the *bolsa* posed a potential threat. Milene felt her first responsibility was to God and her Evangelical community. She could not risk letting a health agent, or any state agent, know that she was fostering the two young boys. In addition, her daughter, Denise, had also been informally adopted; Denise's adoption was also arranged through the Evangelical Church. It is not certain whether the health agents would have cared that Milene was fostering these children. What is certain is that Milene was fearful of what *could* happen if this information was exposed. For Milene and Ana, and others like them, letting the health agents into their homes to be registered to earn the *bolsa* each month was not worth the risk. This was a dangerous option that could open them up to the potential violence of the state. Milene explained, "The government thinks we need them, that we will take anything from them and be happy. But we are strong here; we are not weak like they think we are. For everything I need I can depend on God, here on Earth and in heaven. I once was lost, but now I am found."

The spirit of gifting, which is key to Evangelical faith in a multitude of ways, is turned upside down here. The *bolsa* is a gift from the state that is refused; it is not a free gift but one tied to forms of surveillance. It is also linked to a kind of political promise that many Evangelicals noted was broken. The *bolsa* has been a central axis of a leftist democratic promise that many noted went unfulfilled: they were no better off, people said, but, more than that, they were only ever recognized as criminals, as undesirables, as the objectionables. The *bolsa* was a gift that might keep them alive, but it was not a real gesture of recognition of their worth and humanity.

Milene's words were, of course, an especially well-worn trope: "I once was lost, but now I am found." For Milene this means that she was no longer among the abandoned, lost to the logics of governance in Brazil. She was not precarious, not in need like the Bolsa Família assumed her to be. While the Brazilian government promised a small monthly subsidy, her Evangelical God promised her grace, prosperity, and wealth beyond this earth. This shift in the experience of precarity is seismic, upturning conventional notions of citizenship, welfare, and the project of statehood. It is impossible to disembed the *bolsa* as a gift from the broader experiences of a state understood as first and foremost intending to harm. The determination to not accept the *bolsa* and the recognition of it as an unwanted gift premised in an undesirable exchange is key. The Evangelicals I worked with placed the *bolsa* in a relation of exclusion and harm that they refused. Their refusal was a way to give grace to themselves and extend logics of recognition and value to themselves in ways that might potentially escape the state.

REJECTING BOLSONARO?

The state, in its multiple manifestations, is cunning in its capture. In early 2020, just before the crisis of COVID-19 swept dramatically across Rio, I sat with Jovina on the small patio at her family-run restaurant, like we had done many times before. I had come to spend a few days at their place. It was the longest I had gone without visiting—more than a year—and so everyone treated it like it was a homecoming celebration. Everyone was disappointed that I hadn't brought my kids. As we sat in the early evening sun, we poured over photos and videos together. Elisa sat with us too. She was pregnant again, with a girl, and was due to give birth any day. She looked radiant and healthy. In the time that I had been away, in 2018, the community pacification policing force had been removed, and I was curious to know how Batan was changing. I'd heard from many people that the community was now struggling with the return of trafficking violence, but Jovina dismissed this, saying that so far not much had changed.

"What do you think of Bolsonaro now?" I asked. "Do you still support him?" In 2018 Jair Bolsonaro—a Far Right, conservative, former-military officer—became president of Brazil. After Luiz Inácio Lula da Silva's handpicked successor, Dilma Roussoff, was ousted from office amid a corruption scandal that rocked the leftist political institution Partido dos Trabalhadores (Workers' Party, known as the PT) to its core—and even saw Lula himself jailed—the people elected Bolsonaro on a wave of campaign promises premised on a tough-on-crime agenda and substantially bolstered through Evangelical media, social networks, and funds. In the span of just three elections, the political landscape of Brazil had changed dramatically.[4]

Two years earlier Jovina had been an ardent Bolsonaro supporter and planned to vote for him. This in itself was surprising, as Jovina had abstained from voting for most of her adult life. But during the period leading up to the election, Jovina and other Evangelicals in Batan consistently repeated their support for Bolsonaro. They claimed that Bolsonaro, unlike other politicians, just *felt* different than the politicians they were used to. He was clearly led by God, they said, and in a political landscape that had failed them so often, at least this was a chance at something distinctive. If in their hearts they still held space for Lula the man, they explained, they were nonetheless tired of his party politics. They made it clear that they felt that the Left had done very little to alter or transform their lives for the better. In the city they felt worse off than they'd ever been, piecing together work, barely getting by, with their lives still marred by pervasive racialized violence. Maria José de Abreu (2021) writes on this shift in politics more broadly, identifying the forms of impoverishment and extremism that we can locate Brazil's turn to the conservative Right within, including its political temporality and horizons defined by an aerobatic politics in "gymnasium Brazil."[5]

In answer to my question, though, of whether she still supported Bolsonaro—two years later—Jovina immediately denounced politics more generally. Her husband, who had been behind the counter, came and planted a chair firmly in front of me. He sat down and began speaking angrily. He and Jovina alternated in telling stories about what a failure all politicians were, how they are all were filled with lies. They pointed up the street to the house of a young woman I knew well and told me about her son born with severe disabilities a few years back: "Where was the help for that child?" they wanted to know. They explained that everyone in their Evangelical community took turns caring for the child, shared their food with his mother, and found ways to cover her rent but that she was only ever barely able to get by and constantly had to battle for attention and assistance in the hospitals or from physicians who seemed uninterested in her son's life. "What kind of life is this?" they asked me.

Bolsonaro, they said, was no different than any other politician. He was just like all the others and didn't seem to care about the lives and futures of them and their neighbors. Jovina slumped in her chair and put her head in her hands as the story unfolded. But then she popped up and laughed, "I know, they can collect the *bolsa*," she said, meaning the Bolsa Família. As she laughed, she earnestly repeated a conservative talking point, telling me that the *bolsa* was a scam: "Corrupt and lazy women are living in big homes, having babies and collecting the *bolsa* each month," she told me. Their general lack of trust in the *bolsa*, as an extension of their lack of trust in politics and in the state itself more generally, was not new. But speaking of the *bolsa* in this way—deploying conservative talking points that would be at home in the United States—was something I had not heard before. While Bolsonaro the man and politician was being derided, his conservative principles of self-sufficiency and derision of welfare initiatives, which he rode on a wave of Evangelical prosperity doctrine, were still being expounded. The *bolsa* was still a questionable and corruptible gift.

As we finished talking, we turned our attention to the small, family-only evening church service being prepared in Jovina's small flat, next to the restaurant. Jovina's daughters were setting up, arranging chairs, preparing food, and organizing music. They hadn't called a pastor in for the evening; Jovina would lead us in prayer. I left the patio with Jovina, Elisa, and her other daughter, Mayara. As the sun went down, we moved inside to gather together, holding hands as we stood in a circle. Our intimate service was emotional, a celebration of friendship and faith over the years. Jovina held us together with her powerful preaching; she reached up to the heavens with her voice, cajoling each of us to always stay with Jesus. "The work is clear," she says. "Find Jesus, listen to Jesus, and let Jesus into your heart. Each of us have a future with Jesus." She moved through the circle, kissing each of us on the forehead, gently cupping our faces in her hands as she did so. She spoke directly to each of us that night, asking God for what she thought we needed right now: family, home, health. Her words were detailed, full of care and attention, attempting to direct us through our own thorny mazes. Friendship and family bound us together in this circle. We felt at home with one another. Jovina stepped into the middle of the circle and, praising God, began to cry. It had been a hard two years; her and her husband were struggling, and they were contemplating divorce. Elisa and Mayara and I moved in to hold her. We embraced, both collapsing and augmenting the prayer circle itself. It gracefully held.

THE CONNECTIVE TISSUE OF THE STATE

In *Progressive Dystopia: Abolition, Antiblackness, and Schooling in San Francisco,* Savannah Shange charts a project of state recuperation through the metaphor of the "meniscus," wherein civility is the cushion that allows progress to keep moving forward, a progressivism that is "fundamentally a deconstructionist politic embedded within liberal logics—it aims to hold the state accountable to its promise of democracy and justice. . . . Its story is fundamentally a state romance—'social justice' means living happily ever after with the antiracist, distributive state" (2019, 4). Shange reminds us, however, that this civility is incongruous with Black life in the "afterlife of slavery" (Hartman 2019). Where Blackness is marked as always expendable and uncivil, "lives are always swept up in the wake produced and determined, though not absolutely, by slavery" (Sharpe 2016, 8). The muscles and joints of the state body are seemingly forever being coddled and smoothed out: every harm is excused through deferral. The good state, always on its way, will save. AbdouMaliq Simone (2019), however, directs us to "the hinges" within that body of the state: the rhythms "of endurance, of surging forward and withdrawing. It is not a rhythm of endless becoming nor of staying put; it is making the most of 'the hinge,' of knowing how to move and think through various angles while being fully aware of the constraints, the durability of those things that are 'bad for us'" (Stoler 2016, cited in Simone 2019, 8).

Shange's "abolitionist anthropology" might be a kind of hinge too: a "necessary conjuncture of anti-Blackness theory and critical anthropology of the state" that attends to abolition, not as a "synonym for resistance" but instead as it "encompasses the ways in which Black people and our accomplices work within, against, and beyond the state in the service of collective liberation." Shange continues, "In the process of unthinking the state," an abolitionist anthropology is "a provocation to *care* more than we can *know*, to extend our analyses past the ruins of the world (and the discipline) as we know it" (2019, 7, 10). Maria José de Abreu's writing on the conservative right-wing state's political muscles, joints, and elasticity in Brazil, as embodied in Bolsonarismo, is important in this project of thinking through the formations of state power, both affective and material in Rio today. "At stake" in Brazil, writes Abreu, "is a form of power that draws energy and political shape not from moving toward a specific goal but by running, like an athlete in training, after itself. Such power goes nowhere in particular and yet, precisely, makes this lack of motion without telos its own inevitable end" (2021, 17). This, then, is a politics—a gymnastic playground—defined by "intrigue, temper tantrums, interruption and discontinuous utterances, gestural extravaganza, buffoonery, apocalyptic thought, martyrdom, and despotism" (181–82). These acrobatics fashion and contour the muscles in particular ways. Here a liberal apologist of the state in Brazil depends on what Shange terms the "meniscus," but the state is training not the meniscus but rather the tendons of the trigger finger, the engaged abdomen of the choke hold, and the backward rotation of the spine and the twist of the wrist joint as the police body swings the bat. But other muscles are at work too, other joints, other connective tissues, other kinds of gifts.

.   .   .   .   .

Juliana approaches the microphone, and the crowd gathered becomes quiet. While people are here at this service tonight to encounter God, they are also here to work with Juliana. They pause for her as she takes hold of the mic. I am watching Juliana captured on film: the camera shakes a little, and the video quality blurs, but the sound of her voice rises through the street. She is clearly both preacher and prophet, and the people in the audience are hopeful that she will speak to them, give them a message from God. When she sent me the video a few days after the service took place, she told me that her job was to lift people up to Jesus and in so doing to help them release their pain and tension. "The peace they need is Jesus," she says.

The street in the video is dark, but bright lights flood out of the house behind Juliana. Her small congregation, forty or so people, stand in the street outside her home. A few people sit on the white plastic lawn chairs that have been set up on the sidewalk in preparation for tonight. The person filming catches Juliana walking among the people meditatively. As she passes between two people, something in her body alights, and she halts in front of a young man. She grasps him by the shoulders and begins to preach directly to him, a message from God:

> He wants to deliver a project in your hands, with him knowing that you're not prepared. God, he is a being of infinite wisdom, and he does not want to create a vase to break it right after; he wants to create a vase to fill it up afterward. God does not want to use the vase as decoration. . . . Let it be known, if the promise has not yet arrived, it's because God is preparing the time. God is preparing the work. God is forging the character. God is placing you in the position. He can say, "The son of man places you among the people."

At this moment the crowd shouts out and praises God. On the video the hallelujahs drown out Juliana's voice. They holler after each of her sentences, like punctuation marks. Juliana raises one hand up to the sky, and the crowd is subdued again. She places another hand on the man and speaks again, "I don't know what kind of things you were lacking when you got here. I don't know the state of your heart or your life. I don't know how your spiritual life and how your home are. In the path of the voices, your appearance shows one thing: you're smiling to everyone and to the peace of the Lord, but only you and God know everything that is going on in your home, how your son and your wife are doing, but I want to turn that night into day."

At this point her body shoots into spasms that ripple from her toes to her hair. The words that tumble out of her no longer sound like her voice: "You have a lawyer at your place!" she shouts, then continues,

> He is a lawyer and also has the function of judge. He raises and hits the hammer in your favor. When you spread the obedience and the promise of

God, it has to be kept, but it takes time, because God, he is ready to bless you. He is ready to deliver your victory. . . . I want to tell you this night that you're not just someone. You're not someone who follows other people—you follow Jesus. Turn to God! It might be a hard fight, but he is recognizing that you are winning the fight. He is recognizing that you are winning the battle.

Juliana abruptly stops and begins to move through the crowd, once again serene. The young man sits down and begins to pray, and the camera lingers on him for a few moments as he lifts his head and hands to the heavens. Now zooming in on Juliana, the camera shows her moving toward a middle-aged woman. She grasps the woman's shoulders. "My God," Juliana cries out. "God loves you, my daughter. . . . As much as it hurts here, I am sending proof of that inside your home. Praise God if you want to cry. . . . It's hurting. It's hitting you, but God is teaching you. It's hitting you. It's injuring you, but God is teaching you." Juliana begins to moan in pain, "It's hurting. It's hitting, but it's all providence. Today God opens up to you, my dear. It's a renewal, you know. . . . I see over your shoulders a big burden. I think you are so tired from this burden, and you're telling God, 'Take away my burden; take it away.' God is speaking about your shoulders, woman, about that weight, that burden, which is overloading your soul. The Holy Spirit of God is saying, 'I'm tearing it all down.' You still feel tired, but it's okay because today you are renewing your relations with the spirit." Juliana holds the woman who now weeps, and she lays her into a chair, into the arms of other parishioners. The video stops.

A DIFFERENT KIND OF PROTEST

Juliana sent me the video, along with posters of her past and upcoming preaching events, via Facebook Messenger. I had been following Juliana's preaching for some time. In fact, I had already seen the posted videos. This one she shared with me was just one of many. Juliana and I have known each other for almost a decade; we were neighbors in Batan. Almost ten years ago her two young children—a boy and girl—used to play almost every afternoon with my daughter in my apartment. They'd trudge up the stairs to find her after school, and they would spend hours together. When we were neighbors, Juliana was struggling in her marriage with a husband who was consistently abusive. One morning Juliana's daughter appeared at my door, requesting a suitcase. She was supposed to be in school, but she said that she and her mom were going away together on a trip to São Luís. I knew Juliana had lived there before she moved to Rio, and I knew she still had family there. I gave her a suitcase. I realized a few hours later that I'd given her a suitcase with a broken wheel, so I went over to her house to replace it. Juliana and I started chatting, and I asked her about the trip and how long she expected to be gone. She quickly changed her tone and quietly told me that she wasn't coming back. She was leaving her husband. She said she was taking her daughter but not her son. She wasn't sure how she would leave because her husband didn't want to give her the money for the bus. I told her I could give her the bus fare, but she quickly declined the money, confident that she would sort it out herself.

Juliana and her husband fought all the time, and he was often violent with her. She would lock herself in the house for days at a time after a big fight. Everyone knew this because everyone could hear the fights. Juliana also fought bitterly with her mother-in-law, Diana, who lived nearby. Juliana didn't have a job outside the home, and she was supposed to run the small shop that was part of her mother-in-law's house, but Juliana didn't like the job, and she and Diana would get in fights that could be heard from down the street. Juliana and her husband had one of their biggest fights to date the night before she was meant to leave. In the end Juliana didn't leave that night. She claimed she was delaying leaving because her husband promised they could move—they were going to sell their place and move to a new place, away from her mother-in-law. Unsurprisingly, they didn't move. Over the course of the year, Juliana left but came back at least three times. Juliana's preaching now stands in sharp contrast to this woman who once lived in a cycle of abuse. She stands on the street, microphone in hand, trying to lighten people's loads, attempting to guide them to less heavy lives.

I watch Juliana on the screen in front of me, as I play the short video over and over. There are so few ways for Black women to protest in this city, where the consequences of their protests are endlessly dangerous in a murderous state that puts these women in their place. I play the video again. Here is Juliana holding a woman and telling her that God will take her burden. What a thing to promise, I think, that your burden can be cast away, just like that, given over to God. Shoulders can become light again, unclenched, loose, light, with the holy grace of it all. Juliana holds the woman in her arms: two Black women embracing on the streets. The crowd hollers and circles around them, thanking God for these lives.

5 Failures and Demons

It is Good Friday, and I am standing in front of my house with neighbors. A scooter comes flying up the road, threading its way through the narrow streets. The scooter's driver blasts the horn three times, piercing an uncommonly quiet Friday night. The neighborhood kids leaving for church stand around on the front steps in their best clothes. The boys have all the scuffs shined away from their shoes; the girls twirl their skirts. Those who have returned from church already are back playing on the street, harassing me to retrieve more paper and markers from upstairs.

The scooter pulls up in front of the house and Jovina jumps off, surprising me. *"Vamos"* (Let's go), she hollers. She holds out her own helmet toward me.

"Where to?" I ask, shouting from my doorway.

"Let's go to church, yah?" she responds from the street.

I have just returned from a different Good Friday service at Assembly of God with Ana and Milene and their family. I had previously arranged to go to church with Jovina; she didn't show up, so I went with Milene instead. Lina, a neighbor, was preparing a service in her house that I wanted to attend, and I didn't really want to attend another long service in a church. I start to tell Jovina that we can do it another night, but Milene whispers in my ear, "She is suffering, Laurie. Nothing is going well for her. She needs the church in her life. Her daughters have stopped going, you know? Go with her."

With Milene's prodding I step down to the road, readjust my hair, and put on the helmet. I get on the back of the scooter and hold Jovina's waist. Jovina has separated from her husband again, and she's finding work outside the family restaurant. Their relationship has always been a violent one. When she was pregnant with her first daughter, he pushed her down a flight of stairs, which caused her to go into early labor. They always fought like that in the beginning, but, as Jovina got older—and when she found Jesus—she started sticking up for herself: "God wants more for me, right?" she'd say. For ten years they have had an on-again, off-again relationship, marked by periods in which one or the other would move out of the house. And she would fight back. But Jovina said this time was different. He was really gone now. She was really alone now. Tonight she looks worn out and tired.

Jovina had been given the scooter by her employer. She's in her fifties and delivering cheeseburgers and fries for a local restaurant. She put a sparkling pink decal of her name on the back of the scooter. When she showed it to me the first time, she did a little dance in the street. "Have you ever seen an old lady's name on the back of a scooter?" She laughed joyously, reveling in her new freedom and work. But tonight, just after nine o'clock, she seems deflated. She doesn't have any of the regular pep that ordinarily brightens up a street. Jovina is typically the person who is laughing the loudest when things are good and openly weeping when things turn bad. Tonight, though, she is flat—no laughs, no tears, dispirited.

The Evangelical sensorium wafts. It mollifies. It aches. It raises. It also *hardens*. Through lives and their undulations, I follow some of the circulations, heights, and emptiness of salvation and its sensorial tethers. I also consider how deflation and trauma are prayed on and preyed on—or, as Kevin O'Neill (2017) puts it, how Evangelicals make use of crises and trauma to "hunt" nonbelievers. I often saw the ways that Evangelicals deployed their own stories of trauma and pain at the center of their missioning. Hardening often meant a kind of entrapment that deviled the ability to receive—*or give*—grace.[1]

The scooter hums, and we fly through Batan's main intersection, past the local bar and bakery, up a dirt road to the back roads that will lead us halfway to the next community over. I grip Jovina tightly, as dust flies into my eyes—there is no eye visor on the helmet—and Jovina's hair blows in my face. Jovina moves backward on the seat, making it easier for me to hold on to her. She grips the handles of the scooter and leans sideways as she makes a sharp turn. We merge onto Avenida Brasil but ride on the bumpy shoulder, not the crowded highway itself. Buses, transport trucks, and passenger vans hurtle down the roadside, and we are forced farther onto the dusty side when they stop on the side of the road to hail prospective riders. The copilots hang their bodies out the passenger-side windows, hollering their destinations: Campo Grande, Bangu, Vila Kennedy, Vila Aliança, Seropédica.

We follow almost the same route that Ana and I traveled when we pushed the cart filled with disinfectant. We use an overpass to cross over the highway to Vila Vintém, passing idling taxicabs, with their drivers smoking and sipping small coffees. We pull up on Vintém's main street and get caught in the fluorescent glow of a large Evangelical church. The church assembly hall is a massive room with what looks like a storefront entrance. However, instead of doors there is a nearly fifty-foot open entrance. We walk up the steps and enter the church. We can see the worshippers from the street, and the music takes up every inch of this block's sound space. The tiled and concrete room and wide-open front serves like a loudspeaker to the surrounding community. The congregation sings, reading the words projected on a white screen, accompanied by the electronic instrumental blaring from the sound system. A group of women wearing purple skirts and sashes sing into microphones:

Ele e o Leão da tribo de Judá	(He is the Lion of the tribe of Judah)
Jesus tomou nossas cadeias e nos libertou	(Jesus took our chains and set us free)
Ele é a rocha da nossa vitória	(He is the rock of our victory)

We arrive a little late; the service has already begun. The church is the size of a small department store, and we try to sneak up the right-hand aisle and take our seats quietly. Jovina begins to sing loudly. She does not have to read the words on the screen, so she squeezes her eyes shut while she sings. Her skin drips with sweat, and her glasses keep slipping off her nose. The oversized fans mounted on each side of the room hang limply. I've been here before; I've not once seen them working. Jovina raises her hands in the air and takes my hand and lifts it up with hers. I move my mouth. The young women volunteering as ushers notice us, and they squeeze themselves down the aisle toward us. When they reach us, they pull us in close to embrace. Their polyester blue vests—identifying them as God's helpers—are rough against our skin. Their lips press against my cheeks, and they whisper hotly in my ear their *obrigadas* (thank yous) and *beijos* (kisses) for joining them tonight. My accented *obrigada* makes them pull back. I'm different, a novel different. Jovina stands taller and smiles as she notices them noticing me.

"Where are you from?" they ask.

"Canada," I respond.

"The United States?" they counter.

"No, she is from Canada," Jovina answers definitively. "She is writing a book about the *subúrbios*."

"Come stand with us up front," they giggle.

I politely decline the invitation and stick with Jovina in our row. The young women give me more kisses and move back to their places against the wall near the front of the church, watching for people who may need help and ready to assist the pastors in any way they can. The room is just half-full, with about 150 people in attendance. The service will last at least two hours. The pastor preaches loudly to us from a large, carpeted stage. He paces while he speaks into his microphone, dragging the cord across the floor behind him. "Easter is about passage. Easter is your passage. God is a door. God is a window. God is your way. God is your neighborhood. God is your family."

He preaches on a familiar topic: God is asking for *you*—not somebody abstract and impersonal—but *you*. God is asking you to step out of the boat and walk on water. He tells the story of Jesus and his disciples in their boat during a heavy storm; he then tells us that we too can walk on water with God. "Don't stay in a sinking boat," the preacher hollers at us. "Walk toward God!" he commands. Then he reminds us that "the disciple Peter had little faith—to the face of God, Peter yells, 'save me,' and even he of little faith is saved." He repeats the important parts of the story numerous times, over and over, and beseeches us to turn to God: "You who have nothing, not even faith, can still be saved. Ask God NOW to save you!"

Many people in the room holler to the sky, weeping loudly and shouting out prayers to God. The pastor stands on the stage, now very still. He leans over his lectern and begins to read the story of Jesus arriving at Herod's Temple at Passover. After reading the verses, the pastor's voice drops, barely audible. He whispers softly into his microphone, and I can't quite make out what he is saying. Then his voice begins to rise, a building crescendo that culminates to rock the room as he bellows the final line of this passage: "Jesus answered and said to them, 'Destroy this temple, and in three days I will raise it up.'"

A frantic energy takes over the room. The ushers scatter throughout the church. They approach us from all directions. They herd us toward the front of the church and push us together into a throbbing cluster. My body is pushed right up close to the people around me. A woman behind me leans on my back, and I feel her hot breath against my neck. We seem to be panting together in unison, as a group. We are pushed up front, clustered at the edge of the elevated stage, where the preacher hovers over us. A small boy—maybe seven or eight years old—dressed in a formal blue suit takes the stage and a microphone. He begins to roar like a lion. The sound is so unexpected from the small child that the crowd takes a collective breath, our bodies rocking in sync to the preacher's sermon, still ongoing. As the boy roars into the microphone, he takes huge steps across the stage, back and forth, back and forth. The preacher quiets down, and now the young boy commands us, waving his arms and wagging his finger, encouraging us to roar like lions ourselves: to wrestle with the lion inside us, to defeat our own personal lion. We are bigger and stronger than the demons inside us, he screams. He shouts at us to burn down our temples—to tear out the lion inside us all. He lectures us on the harms that we do to ourselves, to our families and neighbors. He admonishes us about our prideful ways and our false idols. The ushers move between us and distribute small sheets of paper with a picture of a giant lion roaring with teeth bared and the accompanying text: "Venha rasgar o leão que está na sua VIDA" (Come and tear out the lion that is in your LIFE). The young boy tells us to close our eyes and to *devour* our lion.

Another, older pastor now takes the stage with the boy, each with their own microphone, and they growl and roar and wave their arms frantically, imitating a lion that mangles its prey. The ushers approach each of us again. A young woman, short and slight, and wearing a blue apron, comes up to me and grabs my head. She squeezes my scalp and pulls at my hair while chanting, "Tear out the lion! God, tear out the lion! God, tear out the lion!" She pulls strands of my hair from my head and squeezes until I cry out in pain and fear and confusion. Then she embraces me, content that my scream was a demon leaving my body. She moves on to the next person. I am sweating profusely at this point. I turn to Jovina and notice that she is suddenly weeping next to me. The pastor and the boy stop growling after many of us shout out. In each of our screams we shed our lions, our demons. Demons take flight from our bodies. But Jovina does not shout out in pain. She calls up to heaven and asks God for help, but no demons leave her tonight. This is why she now cries.

The older pastor takes the center of the stage. He calmly says into the microphone in a composed and authoritative voice, the antithesis of a growling lion: "The lion will destroy you like prey if you don't defeat it first. Amen." It sounds like a warning shot. This is cold, distinct from the heat he seemed to generate moments ago. The group of us move back to our seats. We sing a few more songs, and then it is time for "seeds." We are meant to buy seeds, to make a monetary sacrifice in front of everyone. The preacher urges us to sacrifice so we can later harvest the blessings of God. Jovina sacrifices fifty centavos and urges me to sacrifice too. She hopes I will sacrifice a lot. The ushers approach me and urge me to sacrifice, but I do not. Jovina shows her frustration by turning her back to me. She wants me to sacrifice, to do the things that I should do—that is, if I have faith.

She has worried out loud to me that all my blessings might not really be blessings. Usually people interpret my clear wealth and prosperity as proof of being chosen by God. But tonight Jovina looks at me suspiciously. She turns her back to me and says, "Just five reais, yeah?" This is an amount she has figured out is nothing to me; it would be huge here in this moment. "I don't want to tonight," I say firmly, not wishing to negotiate with her on the value of my salvation here in public. She keeps her back to me for a few more moments, but then her muscles relax, relenting to my inability to do things the way she wants. "You sacrifice in other ways, actually," she says, taking my hand and letting me back into her fold.[2]

ON THE BROKEN BODY AND FRACTURED SOUL

Elisa and I lie together on her bed, watching cartoons for hours. I fetch us cereal, coffee, and sweets, as we pass the hottest hours of the day indoors with the curtains drawn to block out the sun. At lunchtime I run downstairs and return with hot bags of food in shiny tinfoil from her family's restaurant. As she sits there with me, Elisa still barely talks. Only a few months have passed since the death of her day-old infant daughter. Elisa is depressed, grieving, at a loss. What will become of her life? What could it ever be again?

As we are watching television one afternoon, Elisa's sister, Mayara, bursts into the room. Elisa doesn't even move. Mayara pulls me to my feet and demands that I enter the small kitchen with her. She tells me in a whisper that Danilo—the father of Elisa's baby—is going around and telling everyone that Elisa is to blame for the baby dying. He's saying that she was doing drugs while she was pregnant and selling sex in exchange for cocaine. There are cartoons blaring in the background that should have drowned out Mayara's hushed words, but Elisa yells out at us from four feet away: "Is she telling you what Danilo is saying about me and Megan?"

Elisa gets out of bed and walks across the room. She sits on the floor outside the kitchen with her knees up against her chest, her arms wrapped around her legs. I nod and tell her I've only just heard now, from Mayara, and that I hadn't heard the rumors before. Elisa curls up on the ground, one half of her body pushed against the cold cement floor. Mayara and I curl up on the floor with her, goose bumps appearing on our skin. We all lay there silently for a long time. Our bodies curl in to each other, wrapping up Elisa. Mayara rests her head on Elisa's ribs. Elisa now repeats the rumors to me, whispering, "Danilo is telling everyone that it wasn't a urinary tract infection but drugs and sex that killed Megan. People are believing him."

Mayara swears and calls Danilo a weak man and a liar. She says, "Elisa, he is telling people that you've been in Vila Vintém." The detail about Vila

Vintém makes Elisa shake and she says *"mentiras, mentiras, mentiras"* (lies, lies, lies). Her body stops shaking, and she just lays there, near unconscious on the floor. Mayara and I work together to pick her up and move her to the bed. I could have done it on my own. She has lost so much weight. We all doze in the afternoon heat.

When I wake up, it is past five o'clock, and Jovina and Mayara are watching television in the room. Jovina makes us all coffee, and I sit with Elisa on the bed. Elisa sits up to drink the coffee and starts talking about the rumors, saying that it is all because of her past. Elisa explains to me that she lived in Fumacê—a nearby public-housing block—for two years with a boyfriend who was a trafficker. She had met him when she was selling clothes for her mother. At the time Batan was controlled by the competing drug-trafficking organization. One could not easily walk back and forth between Batan and Fumacê. Space and reputations are intertwined. Elisa says she should not have gone there to sell clothes, but she knew a woman there, and she really needed to make some money. She was eighteen at the time, seven years ago. Once everyone knew she was with him, she was faced with a choice: either move to Fumacê or break up with her boyfriend, as she couldn't easily see him if she lived in Batan.

Mayara laughs at Elisa's old story, saying, "Traffickers used to be the best to date." She starts listing all the good things about them: respect, cars, money. But then she trails off, her fingernails tapping the side of her cup in annoyance. "But they all had fifteen women. . . . We would all go to parties, drink too much."

Elisa chimes in and continues, "Everybody in Batan knows this. That's why Danilo is saying Vila Vintém, because people would believe it. It makes them think about everything I used to do. I probably am doing it all again, they think."

Though Vintém is just across the highway, the politics of its governance are different than in Batan. Vintém has seen numerous organized crime-related conflicts over the years, related to the governance and management of the area. Many of the street entrances are barricaded by boulders and tree trunks, blocking entry to any unknown visitors. At the time the *dono da favela* (favela boss) was actually female—a *dona da favela*—a local woman who took control of trafficking after her husband was jailed. Stories of her group of military-clad and gun-wielding drug trafficking women are notorious. She was arrested in 2019; she is still in prison. At the time of my research, however, Vintém's governance was distinct from much of the western suburbs, which were controlled by militias made up of off-duty police officers and firefighters. While Batan was governed by a Pacification Police Force, its connections to the militia were well documented and enduring. Vila Vintém, which sits outside of this order, is a community that is reviled by Evangelicals because of the perceived scourge of drug use, trafficking, and sex work. However, it is also an important spot for ministering to these people. It is a mission site, a community to be mined for potential believers: a salvific "quarry" (O'Neill 2017, 705).

By placing Elisa in Vintém, Danilo was connecting her and her reputation to a reviled place where only sex workers and drug dealers reside. If Elisa wasn't there for ministry—to give or receive—then there can only be problematic reasons for her having been seen there: reasons that make her dangerous to both herself and others, including the baby. To say that Elisa was seen in Vila Vintém is to say that she opened herself to the demons of drugs and sex, and her daughter's death was therefore her fault.

Less than a month after he started the rumors, Danilo confessed to making them up. He came to Elisa and her family and apologized. He told me a few months later that he wanted and needed to "make everything better." He started babysitting Mayara's daughter after school and helping Jovina with her new small business (selling fitness clothes). And Elisa's family—led by Jovina—took him back in with open arms. They had previously embraced his complicated past, and these lies and rumors were forgiven in much the same way. With demons in the body, poisoning his mouth and ears, Danilo had spread these malicious lies, they said. He had been unable to hear God, they said.

"HALF-DEAD" ON A STOLEN BICYCLE

Danilo is a former drug trafficker from the nearby public-housing complex, Guadalupe, a tall cement structure made up of multiple blocks. The blocks look as though they float in the air. Each one rests on large staircase pillars, with parking underneath. The backside of one of the blocks faces the main highway that runs through the west side. The first time that

Danilo and I speak formally about his past, we are sitting together in Mayara's small apartment, about five months after Megan died. Jovina and Mayara are in the house too. Mayara straightens her hair as she stands in the bathroom door. She pops in and out of our conversation, frequently adding her opinion on something. Danilo is muscular and rarely smiles. He sits stiffly on the sofa, like he might be physically unable to ever fully relax. He rotates through a collection of T-shirts with anime-inspired naked women stretched provocatively across motorcycles or trucks. I've spent a lot of time with him as we've come to work together on a variety of informal businesses in the community. He is often the driver in these pursuits, taking me and other women around the city to find the best deal on items for them to sell. He is stoic and quiet on these long drives, indulging us with our music choices in the car and our incessant chatter and whims. Later he tells me that he is still atoning for what he did to Elisa, for the lies.

Today we have come to Mayara's house for him to tell me about his past. He wants to help me with my project, he tells me rather earnestly. I think I make him nervous with all my questions; he leans in with a mixture of cautiousness, curiosity, and sweetness as he tries to understand my accented Portuguese. He is not flirtatious. He takes the questions seriously, but he is hesitant as he deliberates on how much to share. Mayara and Jovina listen to the halting nature of our conversation, and they begin telling stories about Danilo to put him at ease. These women are his family, even though he is no longer with Elisa. Despite his temporary betrayal, he comes to all family events, eats lunch with them, and does favors for everyone. They prompt Danilo with stories to tell me from his past. Their voices open him up, and Danilo speaks more freely. He begins with a description of himself using drugs at a railway station near Guadalupe just before he quit. He describes it as a moment when he thought he was going to die, but the mood of the story isn't sad or angry. Instead, he laughs about it—making fun of his former self and eliciting laughter from the group of us:

> I started selling drugs, and then I started using them, which meant I had to hide away at the train tracks to use—I couldn't let the other traffickers know I was using. I started first with marijuana because a friend was using it, and I wanted to try. But then I started using other drugs too. I was injecting. I

never got beat up by the police or traffickers because . . . there are places where you can use and places where you can't use. I always stayed in the places where you could use. Down by train tracks, under that highway pass near the block. One night I was almost dead already—I was half-dead—and then I took more, and I could feel my blood pressure rising. I knew I was half-dead, and I was going to be all dead. So I stole a bicycle, and I rode as fast as I could, almost falling off the bike.

Danilo pantomimes riding a bike while "half-dead." He runs back and forth across the small room, bumping into a table, as he demonstrates how wobbly and haphazard it is to ride a bicycle while high. Jovina and Mayara howl with laughter. The conversation continues.

DANILO: So, I rode to the hospital. I was half-dead. I got better in the hospital, and I just stopped the drugs. I decided to never use drugs again. It was that simple. I still drink, but I don't use drugs. . . . They keep the drugs in the favelas to keep the people half-dead.

LAURIE: But how did you leave trafficking and drug use and not get in trouble for that? I thought you couldn't just stop selling?

DANILO: You can't sell drugs and use drugs if you are just a young trafficker. Nobody knew I was taking drugs. But if you want to leave, good. No problem. Just stop selling drugs. He doesn't care if you want to leave. But how will you be a man with money and power if you leave? How will you make money? How will you keep your woman? Those are the things that you have to think about.

JOVINA: This is why you have to answer God when he calls. God will do this for you. God will give you your life and job.

DANILO: Yeah, I know a guy who stopped using drugs and found a job because he answered God.

Danilo explained that he had to leave Guadalupe if he wanted to stay out of drugs. He moved to a nearby community because of the *milícia* that had been in control of it. The *milícia* had strict codes about drug use, and he wanted to stay off drugs. When this conversation took place, Danilo hadn't yet been baptized and was attending church only to "see what it is like." Danilo started going to church with a friend and said he was using my project to think about his past, so he could transform and "fix things for Elisa." Two years later, on a subsequent research trip, Danilo tracked me down to tell me some big news: he had been recently baptized. He said, "It wasn't a big fancy baptism . . . but a baptism. I'm a believer now. You're staying with Elisa, right? Do you see how well she is doing?" He was linking up the stories—of Elisa's suffering, his rumors, and now his conversion. "Elisa is doing really well. . . . You see she has a job; she's healthy, and she looks good again too? And me, I've answered Jesus." I asked Danilo how his conversion happened. He first gave me the usual response—"I heard Jesus's call"—but he later elaborated. A pastor had helped him hear Jesus's call by sharing his own story of failure and involvement with traffickers. Danilo said, "I didn't really know that someone like me *could* hear Jesus."

ON FAILURE AND WORTH

After the Good Friday service, Jovina and I return to where she has been living since she left her husband. It's a third-floor apartment, above Milene's house, where she once lived as a young mother. It is the house where she once happily raised her children. It is a home, like all homes, built from the dust of good memories and the ashes of bad ones. These steep steps we climb today are the same steps she was once shoved down. She can point to the spot where her head hit the wall. *Clunk. Clunk.* She had built this wall with scraps of this and that. Aspiration turned into plaster, memories she could conjure just by tracing a crack in the wall. A crack in the wall holds her firm, tethering her to a different space and time. A crack in a wall, a bump on a step, the dirt that accumulates in a windowsill: each of these bits can be conjured just by closing her eyes.

Now she has an old, single mattress on the floor with just a sheet. The rest of the apartment is completely empty, except for a few plastic bags with clothes and a few dishes in the kitchen. She moved here only a few weeks ago, and she is hesitant to *really* move in. Jovina collapses on the mattress, clearly embarrassed by her surroundings. She apologizes, and I sit down with her and tell her she has no reason to apologize. She's already lost the high she gained in church; she is back to being flat and deflated. She doesn't cry or shout or pray but just hangs limply in my arms. We sit on the mattress, and she tries to pray. Jovina is a woman who can bring down a house with prayer. She used to hold court over my pregnant belly: she would put one hand on me and one hand in the air. She would raise her head to the heavens and triumphantly declare her prayers in a voice that reverberated down the street. But tonight there are no prayers. She tells me that God has forgotten her, and the demons know it. They are after her, she repeats.

She tells me a story: Two weeks ago she had woken up to find a demon hovering over her while she lay in bed. The demon's eyes were just inches from hers. The demon had taken her own shape—it was the body of Jovina hanging over the body of Jovina. It looked just like her, but taut, thinner, emaciated. The demon even wore Jovina's own clothes—it had dressed in the clothes she had discarded beside her bed before she went to sleep. "Who are you?" Jovina had tried to ask, but she couldn't find her voice. The demon seemed to hear her thoughts and told her not to worry: all she had to do was follow. Jovina tried to swat the apparition away, but it locked her in place with its eyes. For a few minutes she struggled to free herself, palpably aware of her heart beating. She felt it in her ears, her fingertips, her gut. Her body went red with exertion. And then, like nothing, the demon was gone, and Jovina felt herself released as if from a physical hold. Jovina said she jumped out of bed and ran out to her veranda. In the night's air, she breathed deeply. She stayed there for hours, crouched in a ball, watching the bright, yellow door for any hint of shadow, fearing to move a single muscle lest it came for her again.

Then, a few days later she was taking a van ride home to Batan, and there had been a second demon attack. As she had stepped out of the van, all of a sudden her body went cold. Her stomach flipped. Her heart shattered. Jovina knew immediately that the demon had come back for her. On the street, she said, she recognized the demon immediately, though it walked among men and women, undetected by anyone else. This time she could move, and so she weaved through the crowds, flying over the curbs, stepping onto the road to go faster than the people ahead of her were walking. She darted around the corner and the next corner, marking each landmark in her mind to ground herself; she was afraid the demon might snatch her away if she lost her focus for even an instant. Her foot slipped out of her shoe, and she felt the cold cement ground; it scratched a little. She dared to look behind her. There was the demon. It was not chasing her. It merely stood across the road, looking at her. She closed her eyes and sank to the ground in prayer. She stretched up her arms and asked Jesus to protect her. She asked for Jesus, but she says she cannot find him now. Maybe, she whispers to me, all this time she was never saved, never chosen: "Just look—all my life in a plastic bag." Worthless.

FAILING GRACE

In this landscape how does one reckon with loss, rock bottoms, and betrayals? So much struggle and yearning over the desire for grace take place in moments of collapse, when grace seems so out of reach. Things just don't end smoothly; the crash and collision of a dream for mercy turns on a knife's edge into nightmare. The demons were at the door all along. The desire for grace can be all-consuming. Of course, pieces of it will always suffice. But when grace is in short supply or the spirit doesn't move believers, collapse can feel even more detrimental. When so much has been invested and sacrificed for spirit and grace—money, space, time, energy, loved ones—it feels like yet another abandonment when one winds up deflated. A body and spirit collapse. Graceless.

The hunt for, and elaboration of, grace in the city—of which this book makes its ethnographic project—is fought over a landscape designed to harm. It is a landscape marked by fear and haunted by demons that prey on frailty and through predictable vices: alcohol, drugs, gangs. Demons thrive where people have been left both destitute and entirely responsible for themselves. They are blamed and marred at every turn. If they cannot be a lion, stronger and more cunning than the demons, they will be hunted down by them at every turn. It is not enough to be careful; the pastor urges more: predation. Turning into a lion—fierce, powerful, and venerated—is part of the project.

Conclusion

A POLITICS OF GRACE

I sat on my front steps with Ana, Milene, and Mayara. The heat that hung in the air was thick like gristle; it was chewable. But as the sun started to set, we knew that some cool relief would arrive. The streets were busy with people arriving home and kids playing. It was still too early to go to church or for the music to really start, and so we all sat outside, just waiting. We spread out rugs on our front stoop and watched the kids playing. These were nice and easy times, for talking and catching up. Juliana popped by and held us all close to her with a story. We were an eager audience. It was nothing much, but she told her story with great drama and wit. She's a master storyteller. It was a story about the shop being out of what she needed and the shopkeeper being a fool about it, but she delivered it so well that we clung to her words. Most evenings were spent like this, sitting on the front steps, watching our children play, waiting for the heat to settle. This night, long ago now, we laughed.

· · · · ·

One night, around eleven o'clock, Elisa's sister, Mayara, arrived at my door and wanted to come in, asking me if I had my recorder ready.

"Sure," I said, "are you all right? We don't need to record anything if you're just here to talk."

"No, I want you to record this," she said. Mayara came upstairs into the house, while I went and got the recorder. It was just me and my sleeping daughter at home that night. Mayara knew her way around my place, and she walked quickly to our small living room, with windows that faced the street. But she turned off the light when she went in, and drew the curtains.

"Are you ok?" I repeated. "Do you want some water? . . . Or I can get us something from the shop downstairs?"

"No," she said with uncharacteristic force. It was only then that I properly noticed she was crying.

She sat down on my sofa. "Is your recorder on?"

"Ok, yeah, sure," I said, not knowing what was coming.

She started to explain that her boyfriend had beaten her hard that night, and she had gone to the police station to report him. But, during the beating, she'd seen Jesus waiting for her, a pool glistening in the light. She knew, with certainty, that she would survive. She didn't linger over the violence but instead described that vision of a future, intact: she was in a pool with a night's sky above her, and yet she was filled with light. She described the sensation of Jesus being with her, part of her, not having a body of his own. She said that as her body was being beaten, crumpled, pummeled, she was elsewhere with Jesus. His grace washed over her like water. She cried out and then whispered, "I held my breath."

.   .   .   .   .

Many years later Mayara and I are standing on her *laje* (rooftop balcony) in an apartment she's renting on her own for herself, her daughter, and her mother. From this vantage point we gaze westward. The sunset drapes our bodies. We're dripping wet, as we've just come out of the temporary inflatable pool she'd set up on the roof to tame the January heat. All day has been a party. The pastor is visiting, and a long service will run through the night. Though the sun is setting, the heat remains. We don't try to dry ourselves off—instead, water pools at our feet. Standing there, looking out, she pulls me to my knees, and she begins to pray.

SENSATIONS OF GRACE

Evangelicals in Rio's western *subúrbios* attune themselves to a felt politics of grace: the sense of hope, optimism, and salvation that the Evangelical promise enables and also, crucially, the ways that this optimism is tethered to a violent conception of the state, its actors and quasi-actors, and its histories and present-day landscapes of racialized and gendered violence, abuse, and pain. This book has traced this fleeting feeling of grace. Grace is something extended—and reached for—when things fall apart. It's often a last gasp, an intake of breath—or no breath at all. The faithful ask for grace in their worst-case scenarios. They need it when it seems like things can't get any worse. In moments of living through extreme duress, at the ends of the rope, it is grace that saves: grace, as the hymn says, is the twin of the wretched.

To give and seek grace in Rio is a rather extraordinary project of refusing present conditions. As Mayara felt each punch, grace was a promise that she would survive, even thrive, despite this incessant violence. Grace is a promise that returns the locus of control, power itself, back to the ones who typically lack power and control. Grace is the promise that God will ultimately bring the faithful home. As believers stand in a prayer circle, holding hands with friends, their shoulders finally unclench after being held tight all day. A prayer circle and the grace of community it offers form a promise—felt in the body—of safety and value, guaranteed by God. Evangelicals say it does not matter how injured, wounded, or broken you are. The grace of God will bring you home safely. For many, grace is a promise of life outside the strictures of worldly violence. If you have not experienced this sensation of grace, it can be difficult to believe that someone might find something of value amid an array of rather kitschy clutter—candles, pulpits, fluorescent lights, plastic lawn chairs—and brassy phrases ("Respond to Jesus's call!" "Open your heart to Jesus!" "I'll pray for you!"). But Evangelicals are insistent they feel God in their bodies, from their toes to their hair. "As I live and breathe," they vow, "Jesus is here with me now."

This grace is complicated too. The longing for grace has been manipulated for decades, if not centuries, by missionaries, pastors, priests, parents, neighbors, friends, and politicians. In particular, right-wing politicians in Brazil have cultivated and used the depth of Evangelical faith and desire, lashing it to a conservatism that claws back rights for the vulnerable and polices race with outright and insidious violence. Religious belief is not harmless, and the forms of violence enacted through Evangelical righteousness—often in the guise of the good—are innumerable through history and not specific to Brazil. And while it offers hope, Evangelical belief is also used to justify all kinds of unbearable harm, including mass murders, urban warfare, the destruction of homes and families, child theft, the implementation of anti-LGBTQ legislation, women's subservience to men, and more. The former president of Brazil, Jair Bolsonaro, mobilized Evangelicalism to usher in a retrograde kind of fascist rule that glorified authoritarianism, embraced militarism, and forcibly suppressed the push for equality.

At the same time, it is clear that Evangelical belief can be intimate and life changing, giving people a sense of power and self-control within a chaotic world. Despite what outsiders see as dangerous fantasy, these felt experiences of grace are spaces envisioned as a kind of emancipation, working against the aches and blasts of violence, both present and past. To go with God is a way to understand present-day constraints on life and to look to something other than policies, politicians, or rights for answers to ongoing violence and poverty.

The experience of Evangelicalism in Rio upends some of the most fundamental assumptions about the city. Evangelicals in the western *subúrbios* often say that they do not live in the periphery of the city. *Periferia,* they say, is a banal misnomer that misses the ways people value and invest in the landscape of the *subúrbios* as one that is both physical and divine. Evangelicals are not clamoring to correct their exclusion from the so-called center of the city; rather, they try to operate outside of these tired terms. If the state, often understood as a homogenous and violent specter, has inflicted devastating violence on their lives, they look elsewhere for value, inclusion, and community. Grace is something that exists in spite of the state but also tethered to it. The search for grace, here in this place, is bound to the violence of everyday life but also exceeds it. By seeking and receiving grace, the often unspoken but ubiquitous question mark that hovers around the concept of *future* (Can we pay the bills this month? Will my son return home tonight? Will my daughter be loved and not harmed?

Will the roof survive the rain? Will the water come back on? Will we stay together as a family?) can be rendered less permanent or even open to question itself.

To reckon with this complicated desire for God and grace, I have tried to place Evangelicalism into the everyday life of Rio by arguing something fairly straightforward throughout: mainly, our understanding of the city is actually enhanced by attuning ourselves to the ways that Evangelicalism has reorganized the felt experience of politics, space, and temporality in the western *suburbios*. These *suburbios* are not new. They are born out of long histories, tied as much to policies—like John F. Kennedy's American Alliance for Progress, which moved the undesirable "antimodern slumd-wellers" far from the city center—as they are to the haunting presence of forced Catholic conversion and the long histories of transatlantic slavery and how it has warped this country. Today, though, when the crises come, when the water fails, when a child dies, when the ground opens up beneath them, recourse is often not demanded in the public square of the city center. Instead, people follow their Evangelical knots and callings. They gather in living rooms converted to small churches, they mourn the unmournable on their bodies with tattoos, and they thank God that the future is on its way, even if the contours of that future are unknowable and literally not of this world. They ask for, give, and receive grace.

To make sense of, and attempt to write down, that feeling of grace and the desire for it, I linger in felt spaces and moments and move slowly through ephemeral sensations and experiences. I consider how particular sensorial experiences make people feel about themselves, about others, about the city, and about the state. I consider times when these feelings are in full flame—like in the midst of a demon-extraction service—and times when it smolders like cinders or vanishes completely, only to reignite and harden again. At the same time, I argue that in these stretches of felt grace, a notion of citizenship has become a far less important goal or benchmark of worth. Seeking grace in the city recognizes that concepts like citizenship and the more typical paths to political recognition—including protests and mobilization—are understood as only partial sense-making vehicles for people who have opted to go with God. Being, or desiring to be, a citizen has proven to be a shaky form of sanctuary in the western *suburbios*. Indeed, the quest for citizenship—which requires being seen and recognized by the state—is often envisioned as an opening to (further) violence for themselves, their families, and their communities. An ongoing uneasiness emerged during my research, which is addressed in this manuscript through the following questions: What is there *besides* citizenship? What other modes of political life are possible, desirable, and attainable? Are they any less dangerous? What do they amount to? Where are the spaces where the wolves are not incessantly biting at your heels?

TUNNELS OF FEELING

The ethnographic work that led to this book has felt at times like being invited to move through a network of tunnels just beneath the surface of taken-for-granted routes through Rio, where angels and demons roam. *Look here! Peer there! Quick, pay attention now!* And rather than attempt a clear and lucid picture, I have opted to write a book reminiscent of travel in these tunnels of feeling. This has led to an analysis and a style of writing that can feel uncomfortable or obtuse, with the reader unsure of where they are or how exactly to feel. I want the reader to experience these sensations, even if that means feeling lost or upended by them. I aim to create an experience for the reader that allows them to both think and feel the kinds of sensations that compel people to believe—the joy in the *whoosh*—but also the kinds of anxiety or discomfort that can be experienced when the desire for grace does not actually result in a feeling of grace: the way that the desire itself can itch your skin, nag you, and relentlessly remind you that you must be nothing because where in the world do you see grace? Tunneling like this, through feelings of desire, euphoria, and loss, produces a patchy work, one that bypasses other ways of knowing, telling, and understanding. A tunnel can't tell a whole story. It is not meant to. A tunnel reveals and obscures, making the landscapes it evades impossible to fully grasp. As such, the stories of people's lives that I tell here cannot be told completely or even accurately. But I hope that I get the feeling and sensation right.

Seeking to convey these kinds of feelings, I compact, fold, and twist lives into something digestible. The word, the page, the book: these are all too small to accommodate the richness of individual lives, but I believe that the detailed descriptions nevertheless open something grander and more expansive. In *The Resonance of Unseen Things*, Susan Lepselter troubles the category of "the real" and what it might mean to think with "the real" (or not) ethnographically. Like her, I am not so much interested in what is real or not real, though it is true that this question—and where I stood on it—mattered to my Evangelical interlocutors. But those discussions with them and others about realness, parsed through a discourse of belief, were less about what side one fell on and more about the anxieties of believing itself, about an ongoing indeterminacy felt in the pit of your stomach over the promises and desires of believing. But Lepselter asks, when listening to these uncanny stories (for her, about UFOs; for me, about angels, demons, and Jesus as well as other divine sensations), "How do you let yourself know, in the theories and stories you are told, the weight of the past or the intimations of the future, and to take them seriously as signs (signs of what)?" The stories I heard and relate are less truths or nontruths, real or fake, than stories that matter, inflected by the everyday life in which they take place. If that is the case, Lepselter continues, then what might matter is how we pay attention to the "shades of the story," where stories are "agitations in the air" (2016, 16, 17).

I am interested in how stories are theories: elaborations on the past, present, and future. How do these elaborations agitate, such that stories come to shift the atmosphere and compel certain kinds of ideals or promises for worlds and futures, while also telling us something about the now: *this* side of the road, *this* smell, *this* touch? In *Go with God* I have considered what kind of ethnographic knowing unfolds in moments where you allow yourself to be agitated by an elaboration—from a preacher, from a roadside angel, from a demon prowling the street, from the smell of the divine, from a fallible ethnographer.

.   .   .   .   .

As I scoop up a cup of fragrance to pour into Milene's funnel, to slip down the little green tube into a plastic bottle, she asks me again the name of my baby—the one I am pregnant with. I tell her again that we aren't sure, and she tells me again that we need to decide quickly, that the baby must have a name, especially before we travel. My time living in Batan will soon come to an end, as we are leaving for Canada to have the baby. I'm eight months pregnant, and my physician is writing a note to let me travel, telling them I'm only six months pregnant. My belly is huge in this small room that I have come to know so well. I struggle to twist where needed, to reach for things, to help make the disinfectant. My help today seems more like a scheme, a flimsy excuse to just spend time together. I cannot possibly be useful. Milene's next question to me is about the future: "Are you dreaming about Canada right now?" I tell her yes and no, and we talk about the importance of family, how I want to be closer to my mum when I give birth again. Milene nods in understanding. This is the right thing to do, she says. Milene is in her fifties and has raised three children but has a new house full of young children again—an adopted daughter, two little boys she is fostering from the Evangelical Church, and an infant granddaughter she cares for two weeks out of every month.

"What are you dreaming about?" I ask.

"Oh, I am dreaming about getting out of this room," she laughs. And then she continues, pausing and savoring each word: "A house with a big yard. . . . We could move somewhere here in Batan that has a big yard, like the places around the corner. I could grow a big garden like in São Luís. We'd have lots of animals and fruit trees." But then she suddenly stops and scolds herself—and then scolds me: "We can dream, Laurie, but only God knows. The future is already known. God knows my future, and he is carrying me to it, Laurie. But I can't ask for that backyard. I can't pray to God and ask him for that. I just listen and know he is taking me to it. Maybe there is no backyard for me, but the future is still good. . . . Listen to God and name the baby, Laurie. Do not have doubt in the future."

Notes

"As I staked the soil for the peas this afternoon," Lucia Lorenzi (2021) writes, "I thought about how staking in academia is so often about defensiveness, about occupation. Staking a claim as a settler-colonial act. What if staking could be about offering support for growth? Affixing gently, proximity." I offer up an approach to notes from such an idea: a citational practice premised in making clear from whose stakes and shoots I'm climbing, borrowing, twisting, and growing. These stakes are a form of closeness, rendered through shared words, a traveling quotation, a story lodged in my mind, or a seed that slips into the garden to somehow grow something new and unexpected.

In this way my notes can feel overly long, maybe (b)rambly, and simultaneously incomplete—an underground network of tunnels or a knot of roots holding up a wispy tree. If this manuscript is an attempt to balloon into existence a different way of knowing Evangelicalism, the notes show from whence came the air I breathed to do so. This book, like Lorenzi's spring pea shoots, or my own summer tomatoes, thrive because they both hold tight to their tether *and* reach off somewhere different—with hope they will bear fruit along the way. What I write comes from somewhere; it is staked and planted in specific writers, thinkers, ideas, and experiences.

INTRODUCTION

1. Another way to phrase this is to say that I pay attention to the affective experience of Evangelicalism, or the way it gets felt in the body. Affect draws attention to the ways that bodies are both shifts and tethers. Bodies are shifts, both perceiving and reacting—they bristle, simmer, deflate, and pulse and thus are entry points to understanding the emotionally charged and sensorially rich ways that experiences are generated and lived in bodies. Affect reveals the ways that certain experiences can never be fully named or spoken, even formed, only felt, exceeding the discursive or material realm. They are tethers too. Shifting bodies, tethered to certain histories and landscapes, exceed these contextual binds and openings, but these moor lines remain, revealing how affect unfolds in relation to power. This political and emotional condition of affect is important.

Sara Ahmed (2010, 13) characterizes her approach as a "feminist cultural studies of emotion and affect." For Ahmed, along with Eve Sedgwick (2003), Kathleen Stewart (2007), and Lauren Berlant (2011), feelings and emotions direct bodies through the world. Affects organize how bodies navigate and move. In a feminist conception of affect, the latter cannot be undone from emotion, because, as Ahmed writes, "this analytic distinction between affect and emotion risks cutting emotions off from the lived experiences of being and having a body" (2004, 39). Stewart's *Ordinary Affects* picks up on this emotionally charged and sensorially rich way that bodies move within and encounter the world: "We will follow any hint of energy. . . . When something happens, we swarm toward it, gaze at it, sniff it, absorb its force, pore over its details, make fun of it, hide from it, spit it out, or develop a taste for it. We complain about the compulsion to participate. We deny its pull. We blame it on the suburbs and TV and ourselves. But we desire it, too, and the cure usually another kind of swarming" (2007, 70).

Stewart, building from Berlant's notion of optimistic attachments, suggests that these affective attachments suffuse and constitute "worldings," or what she calls the "bloom space." For Stewart this bloom space is a process across space: an affective saturation of the body in specific landscapes of power and history or across bodies and worlds. In her words, the space is "an allure and a threat that shows up in ordinary sensibilities of not knowing what compels, not being able to sit still, being exhausted, being left behind or being ahead of the curve, being in history, being in a predicament, being ready for something—anything—to happen, or orienting yourself to the goal of making sure that nothing (more) will happen" (2010, 339, 340). For both Stewart and Berlant, this magnetism is sensual. Here, the bloom space resembles the body reading the atmosphere in a room (Brennan 2004, 1), but *queered*, as Ahmed explains. The atmosphere is not a unidirectional force that impedes the body. Rather, the body is always already something; it arrives "moody," and that moody body is then folded into spheres and regimes of possibility, the "messiness of the experiential, the unfolding of bodies into worlds . . . how we are touched by what comes near" (2010, 40, 22).

Throughout this book I am drawn to the very literal meaning of this. When Ahmed writes about affect and "what comes near," she is speaking literally too. And so I find Nicholas Shapiro's work linking toxicity, atmospheres, and affects to be crucial to my argument too. Writing on the ways in which bodies are always entangled in their atmospheres and compelled to do the first-order sensory work of encountering toxic landscapes, Shapiro notes the specific entanglements of bodies and pollutants in "late industrial material ecologies" as well as the ways that exposure is often not an emergency but a slow-paced, mundane encounter with toxic leakages. As he notes, what comes near us is about the circulation of bodies and materials in spaces that are structured in particular ways (2015, 369).

The Evangelicals I write about live and seek grace in a *subúrbio* open to the leakages of industrial and late-liberal waste, defined by a condition of political abandonment, where state presence is often felt often through absence or force. As Sharad Chari (2017) writes, this is life amid toxicity, "a politics of dwelling in the detritus of racial capitalism, and a reaching for the poetry of the future."

2. This book takes place in the western *subúrbios* of Rio de Janeiro, mostly in Batan and the surrounding communities scattered up and down the main highway, Avenida Brasil, which bisects this part of the city. Batan has become an exceptional place in Rio's western *subúrbios*, and, in telling some of Batan's residents' stories, I cannot reasonably expect to hide Batan behind a pseudonym. Some of the reasons why—particular state interventions and an incident of global significance, for example—will become clear throughout the chapters.

The western *subúrbios* are about twenty-five miles from Rio's downtown center and the South Zone (Zona Sul). These twenty-five miles that separate the prestigious and well-known South Zone from the northern half of the western side is a complex of congested highways and shopping malls and is dominated by favelas—formally demarcated or not—built on Rio's flatlands. These twenty-five miles can routinely take two and a half hours to cover, usually with at least three modes of "public" transportation (bus, metro, and a van operated by private security militias).

The West Zone (Zona Oeste) of Rio de Janeiro is a large administrative zone divided by a number of mountain ranges. What I demarcate as the "western *subúrbios*" in this manuscript is the piece of the West Zone located on the northwest side of the mountain range before Jacarepagua. This distinction holds the western *subúrbios* apart from the globally infamous City of God favela and the elite neighborhood Barra de Tijuca, which are also formally designated as part of the West Zone but are not typically included when the word *subúrbios* is used. My demarcation is subjective and likely flawed, but the *subúrbios* are far too big to take as a monolith anyway.

3. Research on religious life in the city shows that Evangelical churches draw the majority of their new adherents from poorer areas of the city (see Lanz 2016; Oosterbaan 2006; Vital da Cunha 2009a, 2009b). Brazil is, of course, famous for the emergence of the Igreja Universal do Reino de Deus (Universal Church of the Kingdom of God). Founded in Rio in 1977, it is a branch of Pentecostal and Charismatic Christianity, often categorized as neo-Pentecostalism.

The IURD is characterized by the prosperity doctrine, which holds that all people have the God-given right to prosperity, in terms of material, physical, and psychological health. This prosperity gospel is often coupled with a doctrine of spiritual warfare, where one is considered to be in constant spiritual combat with demons that block the paths to prosperity. Accordingly, if you experience ill health, poverty, or unhappiness, this is because of demons who must be battled, through prayer, healing ceremonies, demon exorcisms, and sacrificial giving (Freston 1993, 1995, 2001; see also Mariz and Machado 1994; Coleman 2000; Gifford 2004).

At the same time, the IURD does not emphasize gifts of the Holy Spirit (hearing and speaking to God) in the same way that other forms of Pentecostalism do. The IURD plays down most all experiences of speaking in tongues or being filled with the Holy Spirit. Indeed, the Holy Spirit is not central to its theologies, and there is almost no mention of glossolalia. Rather, the Brazilian branches of the IURD focus almost exclusively on rituals that force prosperity-clogging demons from the body and are attuned to very local ideas of affliction and magical forms of intervention (Birman and Lehmann 1999, 154–56; Kramer 2005, 95–113; Oro 1997).

In chapter 2, I outline the ways that everyday Evangelical religious beliefs and practices are far more diverse than the IURD, though significantly influenced by it. I use the term "Evangelical" (in Portuguese, "Evangelico" or *crente* [believer]) because these are the terms the people I worked with used. Joel Robbins (2003, 2004b) has suggested that to develop a more coherent and comparative anthropology of Christianity, a first step is an agreement on terms. For those studying Pentecostalism, broadly speaking, he suggests "Pentecostal and Charismatic Christianity" as a unifying term. I have elsewhere followed this suggestion but found myself later unhappy with this homogenization, especially given what I describe in chapter 2 regarding how people think of themselves, how they attend church, how they think about what a church is, and how their political alliances shift with "Pentecostal-ism" in Brazil.

4. Both Brodwyn Fischer (2008) and Bryan McCann (2014) relate how the spatial formations of Rio's *subúrbios* have actually emerged from calcu-lated state practices of land subdivision and the placement of state-run (and then abandoned) public housing. McCann explains that as the first and sec-ond waves of industrial development rolled forward in Rio, the northern and western parts of the city saw these self-constructed communities expand in step. He argues convincingly that the emergence and endurance of informal communities occur largely because of the desire for them on both sides: the urban poor, often Black migrants from the country's northeast, needed places to live, while the wealthy required supplies of cheap and local labor.

Fischer (2008) and McCann have both documented how, in the late nine-teenth century, Rio's factory workers were often allowed to build their homes behind factories, which was "a solution that guaranteed their employers a local workforce while suppressing wages" (2014, 22). Semipublic institutions such as hospitals and utility providers often did the same (Fischer 2008).

This practice of building on factory land (or very close by) formed part of the informal and underregulated real estate and land-title market that over-whelmingly disfavored Black Brazilians. McCann furthermore explains how, starting in the 1950s and into the 1980s, as populations increased in these parts of the city, irregular *loteamentos* (subdivisions) and self-constructed communities grew as developers bought up land in the expanding areas of the city, divided the lots, and then sold them to families who built their homes there. These land developers themselves had only semilegal owner-ship of the lots, and they rarely registered the subdivided pieces of land with the state or municipality. This meant that families did not have formalized property titles, making them beholden to clientelistic local politicians. Simi-larly, families that had built homes near factories under an arrangement of informal exchange and beneficence found, starting in the 1980s, that they had no formal legal rights to the land that they had called home for more than fifty years (2014, 22–32).

Infrastructure in the western *subúrbios* was and still is an afterthought. In the 1960s and 1970s, new *conjuntos* (public-housing projects) sprang up around these *loteamentos* and self-constructed communities and dotted the landscape with their characteristic style of tall, multistoried cement struc-tures with limited water, sewage, and electric infrastructure. McCann explains how the families and individuals forced into these projects after eviction from centrally located favelas received nontransferable land titles, obligating them to make monthly mortgage payments. These supposedly nontransferable apartments quickly became part of the local informal real estate market. New owners—in many cases, migrants from the northeast of the country with direct links to other migrants in the north and west of the city—did not make the mortgage payments, had no real land-title rights, and were therefore unable to demand that the state maintain its infrastructure promises. Other new migrants then built their homes between and around these *conjuntos*, linking into the unfinished infrastructure (2014, 31–32). Black migrants found themselves owning and building property where almost no infrastructure existed, but they were unable to effectively demand rights to water, sanitation systems, and electricity. (This is taken up in more detail in chapter 2).

5. Nelson da Nóbrega Fernandes describes how the term *periferia* (periphery), as it is used in Brazil, emerged from urbanization processes during the 1960s to 1970s and operates today as a political designation about class and race. The term *subúrbios*, he explains, has become almost synonymous with *periphery*, such that the spatial aspect of it has become irrelevant: "Today, when one says 'suburb,' the word no longer carries its rich polysemy nor does it represent the different forms of use and occupation that might exist in that space, being stripped of its original geographical sense. The peripheral position—the most unchanging element of its history, that which ensures the correspondence between the word and the reality—disappears, being mistaken, replaced by the representation of political, social and cultural distance" (2011, 13). *Suburbios*, then, often acts as a pejorative connotation that codes racialization and exclusion from the city (for further reading, see Pallone [2005] and Maurício Abreu [1987]).

This being said, the term has always been in various ways reclaimed, through music, dance, political organization, and in the everyday language of those who live in these *periferias*. Derek Pardue (2010) and Jennifer Roth-Gordon (2008), for example, have each outlined the ways that people have laid claim to the term to render it differently, giving new meaning and political purpose in contestations over the urban. In Pardue's work, he locates the ways that *periferia* is "an ideological and spatial concept rooted in the artistic expressions of the 'marginal.'"

Through an attention to the use of the term by hip-hop artists in São Paulo, Pardue explains, "In their activities, hip hoppers articulate 'periphery' as not only a place but also as an epistemology, which in turn works to change the meaning of the city for the historically disenfranchised. Not without its limitations and internal critics, marginality secretes a 'magic' or at least retains a pull as hip hoppers and urban, working-class Brazilians, in general, look to convince others of their value in exchange for respect" (2010, 48).

Roth-Gordon's work adds further layers to this by accentuating the ways that the term *periferia* is deployed in Brazilian hip-hop as a means to con-

nect and elaborate on the global specter of the periphery itself and the forms
of violence inherent to them:

> In the rap song *Periferia é Periferia* ("Periphery is Periphery") . . . [the artists]
> take up the example of drug trafficking to explain the marginalization of poor
> Black youth. This song reveals what rappers see as direct parallels between
> their situation and that of the U.S. ghetto (including drugs, structural violence,
> and social inequality). It also draws on these connections, importing the power
> and prestige associated with the U.S. ghetto, attempting to unite the youth of
> Brazil's socially and geographically marginalized communities through a
> refrain of solidarity: *Periferia é periferia* ("Periphery is periphery"). In so doing,
> rappers link marginalized Brazilian spaces to Black America and its location in
> the First World. (2008, 66)

6. In Brazil the Black figure of the *bandido* (criminal) is the imagined
body of threat to Brazil's status quo. It is also the body that functions as the
premise for the formation of the Brazilian state, where the enslavement and
destruction of this "threatening" body literally made Brazil through the logics of slavery and eugenics (Lefèvre 1993; Zaluar 1994; Salem and Robb
Larkins 2021; Hinz and Vinuto 2022).

As Michelle Alexander (2010) has written of the United States, there is a
"new Jim Crow" that continues the same logics of violence and segregation,
but in *palatable* ways that need not utilize explicitly racial language or distinction. This is perfectly idealized in the Brazilian idea of "racial democracy," a dominant discourse of national identity that allows for power to deny
its racial buttresses (Skidmore 1999; Turra and Venturi 1995). And while
this has shifted very modestly under recent government affirmative-action
efforts (Htun 2004), little has changed in people's everyday lives in the city.

Indeed, as Jaime Alves argues, "black participation/exclusion in the public
sphere" is a faulty mode of measurement, where civil society operates "as a
political community that replicates the colonial structure of power even when
including some black and indigenous bodies. Although not homogenously
white, civil society is essentially anti-black" (2018, 3). The *subúrbios* are
defined by anti-Blackness, where the marginal body is central to the urban
imagination in so-called nonracist ways, obscured through the language of
order, security, and respectability and then parsed again through appearance,
documents, address, and livelihood. The *subúrbios* are policed spaces where
Black life is routinely exterminated through police killings and the sly work of
negligence, inattention, and delay.

7. What Jaime Alves explores is the way that in Brazil Black life is rendered
killable. In *The Anti-Black City: Police Terror and Black Urban Life in Brazil*,
he charts this murderous tendency of the state, demonstrating how "spatial
segregation, mass incarceration, and killings by the police are constitutive
dimensions of the reproduction of urban order" (2018, 2). Anti-Black violence

is both organized and organizing—it is a *terror* that is "neither dysfunctional nor [about] failed democracies; rather, anti-black policing creates conditions of possibility for the making of the 'city of man' *[koinonia of politai]*, an anti-black social formation where whites exercise their civil rights" (3). In other words, what Alves shows is that Black life and civil life are imagined within an "antithetical relation," wherein civility requires and organizes anti-Black violence as part of its formation (3).

In the book Jaime Alves (2018) develops a theory of anti-Black violence in Brazil, extending Achille Mbembe's (2019) concept of necropolitics in Brazilian cities and more broadly. Here Alves shows how the concept of necropolitics speaks to the very in-between of life and death that occurs in spaces like the favela, or the transatlantic slave trade, the plantation, and the condition of the colony itself more generally. In attending to the conditions of life and death in Brazil, Alves uses the concept of necropolitics to name white supremacy itself, rather than a diffuse power or system of governance, as the foundation of contemporary ordering and state making.

For Mbembe necropolitics is the "subjugation of life to the power of death," which takes acute racial form. He writes that in "our contemporary world . . . weapons are deployed in the interest of maximum destruction of persons and the creation of *death-worlds*, new and unique forms of social existence in which vast populations are subjugated to conditions of life conferring upon them the status of *living-dead*" (2019, 39–40). Necropolitics are also always necroeconomies, where the bodies of certain populations, and their denial, are reproduced through capitalist conditions of exploitation. Elaborating on Agamben, Mbembe speaks to the way camps—from prisons to *subúrbios* to *banlieues*—are ways of keeping certain populations contained, enclosed, and policed in their precariousness, subject to unpunishable death, and yet still functioning in tandem with contemporary capitalist logics of cheap labor and private property.

In her ethnography of Bahia, Brazil, Christen Smith (2016) explains this dual character of life and death and the spaces in between. Through an attention to how Blackness in Brazil is consumed and celebrated, marketed and capitalized, through tourism projects centered on a reified and exotic Black culture—from carnival celebrations to apolitical capoeira lessons—Smith reflects on how this operates in tandem with unlimited violence; how Black people in Bahia are terrorized and exterminated through routine police killings and other modes of state-sanctioned violence.

Smith terms Bahia an "afro-paradise," a comment on the ways that the fantasy about Blackness—and the way this sells—is intrinsically linked to the limitlessness of Black death, as the celebration is always a fantasy (a paradise): "The atmosphere of violence in Bahia is not in contradiction to the city's identity as a 'paradise.' To the contrary, one cannot exist without the other" (2016, 3). Here Smith uses the concept of necropolitics to explain that logics of governance render "Black people . . . as nonhuman and noncitizen. . . . Consequently, there is no possibility of stripping off legal and moral protection—by definition, to be black means that you exist already without these coverings" (20).

In this way necropolitics is a careful critique of biopolitics and its limits, as well as the mechanisms of bare life. An attention to practices of necropolitics reveals how certain populations are conceived by the state as *already* politically dead. For Smith and Alves, this is central to understanding the political organization of Brazil, where state terror is a genocidal act, premised on the eradication of Blackness in Brazil, while holding onto the parts of Blackness that can be crafted into a commodity to be sold and consumed by tourists.

What scholars like Alves and Smith demonstrate are the limits of a concept like biopolitics for understanding both historical and contemporary modes of governance of "life itself," where the project of the state has always been tied to a politics of death against populations never afforded recognition as humans, let alone citizens, within white supremacist logics. See also the work of Dina Alves (2017); Fábio Alves Araújo (2016); Osmundo Pinho and João H. Costa Vargas (2017); João H. Costa Vargas (2006, 2013); Francisco Paulino Cardoso (2017); Ana Luisa Flauzina and João H. Costa Vargas (2017); Antonio Sérgio Alfredo Guimarães (2003); Maria Aparecida Silva Bento (1995); Ignácio Cano (1997, 2010); Sidney Chalhoub (1988); and Ney do Santos Oliveira (2007).

8. Much work on Pentecostalism in Brazil has linked the flourishing of Pentecostalism to the widespread need to "cope with poverty" (Mariz and Machado 1994), making a clear materialist-based (in the sense of political-economy) argument for Pentecostalism's popularity (see Burdick 1993). More recent analyses based on a logic of "transformation" or "break" are often conceived within a frame that posits that an individualistic ethos inhabits Pentecostalism.

This conception of Pentecostalism is usually part of analyses that link together the rise of Pentecostalism with the rise of neoliberalism (Comaroff and Comaroff 1999, 2000). Here Pentecostalism is read through the lens of a monolithic neoliberalism that emphasizes material prosperity, entrepreneurism, personal achievement, and empowerment, noting that the Pentecostal faith seems to honor and embody these characteristics as well (Machado 2005).

This line of argumentation is often folded into discussions about whether Pentecostalism is an extension of Max Weber's (1905) "Protestant ethic." This view of Pentecostalism seems to at times reduce Pentecostal transformations to a kind of strategy for maneuvering a complex neoliberal landscape. Jean Comaroff and John Comaroff take such an approach. For them Pentecostalism—or, more specifically, the prosperity-oriented neo-Pentecostalism of the Universal Church of the Kingdom of God—is "Pentecostalism meets neoliberal enterprise" or, in their theorization, a kind of occult economy in the postcolony, similar to the workings of witchcraft (1999, 291). In this way the out-of-reach spectral consumption and accumulation within neoliberal flourishing is given magical and occult origins, and those excluded from this flourishing believe that they can use the supernatural powers of a Pentecostal God to attain the same kinds of prosperity.

Others have disagreed with this assessment, instead making sense of Pentecostalisms within their own particular locales, and do not conceive of Pentecostalism as a kind of straightforward outcome of neoliberalism but instead consider the ways that Pentecostalism can be socially, economically, and politically productive (Machado 2005; Bialecki 2009, 2017; Haynes 2012; Robbins 2009; Strhan 2015; van Dijk 2009). Indeed, as Naomi Haynes argues, by knotting together Pentecostalism and neoliberalism, what we are really doing is figuring religion solely "as a super-structural epiphenomenon moving over the solid base of capitalist hegemony" (2012, 125) and barring outright any conception of religion as a "site of *action;* invested in and appropriated by believers" (Marshall 2009, 22).

In this way, Haynes's ethnographic work has been particularly illuminating (2012, 2013). Haynes's (2013) work articulates how the Pentecostal promise of wealth and prosperity is often adjusted to suit the locations and networks in which the promise was made. In her ethnographic work in Zambia, for example, she explores how the promise of prosperity and its links to some kind of universal neoliberalism are interpreted and refracted through experiences of economic uncertainty and already existing modes of social organizations rather than church-imposed or neoliberal-imposed orders.

9. I am thinking here with Ahmed's invitation to consider what a notion of resilience asks of bodies:

> If the twig was a stronger twig, if the twig was more resilient, it would take more pressure before it snapped. We can see how resilience is a technology of will, or even functions as a command: be willing to bear more; be stronger so you can bear more. We can understand too how resilience becomes a deeply conservative technique, one especially well suited to governance: you encourage bodies to strengthen so they will not succumb to pressure; so they can keep taking it; so they can take more of it. Resilience is the requirement to take more pressure; such that the pressure can be gradually increased. (2017, 189)

10. Theologically speaking, grace is the undeserved gift. Central to Christian storying, God arrived not in the form of a vengeful flood or a fiery bush

but in the form of a fragile infant. In this telling God came to Earth vulnerable to understand and embody humanity and in turn to give and extend humanity to a wretched and undeserving people. When the crowds mocked and slandered Jesus and then hung him on the cross, he responded by giving grace rather than vengeance or correction. He bestowed everlasting love and protection: the promise of eternal life.

In Christianity to give grace, then, is to give mercy. To be given grace is to accept that eternal promise of love and graciousness. Michael Edwards and Méadhbh McIvor turn to Martin Luther to define grace in both theology and the everyday: "While grace's theological contours differ depending on the Christian tradition in question, it is usually used to mean . . . 'God's favour, or the good-will God bears us' (Luther 1976, xvi). As such, grace has a peculiar relationship to human agency. Despite its being a form of favour, blessing, or power beyond one's control, one can still be held accountable for its lack" (Edwards and McIvor 2022, 2).

Edwards and McIvor also direct us to Julian Pitt-River's work on grace and offer an analysis of how his broad definition can direct contemporary ethnographies of grace:

> We retain Pitt-River's more general definition of grace. . . . "The only general rule that can be cited," [Pitt-River] writes, "is that grace is always something extra, over and above 'what counts,' what is obligatory or predictable." . . . The value of this capacious definition is that it captures the Christian valence of grace while also directing our attention to a wider set of concepts of interest to anthropologists. Indeed, it is in the encounter between grace and its putative others—law, obligation, accountability, karma, and so on—that the former finds its clearest expression and anthropological potential. An anthropology of grace, we argue, offers much-needed conceptual tools for ethnographers working in spaces where the logics of calculation and accounting are pushed to their limits (if not exceeded), particularly at the intersections of religion, law, and economics. (2022, 2–3)

11. Saidiya Hartman outlines the afterlife of slavery as an ongoing form of violence that organizes the world as we know it today, explaining that enslavement "established a measure of man and a ranking of life and worth that has yet to be undone." In turn "Black lives are still imperiled and devalued by a racial calculus and a political arithmetic that were entrenched centuries ago" (2007, 6). Ashon Crawley's work places Black Pentecostalism within "the violence of the Middle Passage and enslavement, the violence of enslavement and its ongoing afterlife" (2017, 5). Crawley's work expands and expounds on an approach to understanding Black Pentecostal lived practice as always an abolitionist project that exceeds liberalism and the liberal subject insofar that "Black social life, to be precise, is an abolitionist politic, it is the ongoing "no," a black disbelief in the conditions under which we are told we must endure" (6).

Crawley opens this dialogue between Black Pentecostalism and abolition further through his turn to the "otherwise," elaborating "upon the extra-subjective mode of being together that is the condition of occasion for envisioning, and living into such envisioning, a critique of the known—the violent, oppressive, normative—world. The performative practices of Blackpentecostalism constitute a disruptive force, generative for imagining otherwise modes of social organization and mobilization" that defies an insistence on theology, subjectivity, and philosophy as conceived within the liberal project (2017, 4).

12. Others have grappled too with this persistent problem of how to understand and take seriously Evangelical faith alongside the ongoing right-wing manipulation of that depth of faith. There is no easy reckoning here, and I am uncomfortable with binary thinking that doesn't grapple with the everyday messiness of faith and political orientation in Rio. David C. Thompson suggests that these debates at least partly reveal "the heterogeneity of the evangelical movement as a whole" (2022, 11), opening up space for perhaps multiple kinds of truth, from Vilma Reis's (2005) account of Evangelical pastors as pariahs in Salvador, to John Burdick's (1999) attention to Evangelicalism in Brazil as intimately connected to Black identity itself.

13. I am thinking here with AbdouMaliq Simone, who reminds us that in cities "the conditions viewed as uninhabitable produce a series of maneuvers, thousands of small experiments that attempt to provisionally reconcile the demands that residents submerge themselves into the sensibilities connoted by their destitution or expendability" (2019, 27).

14. Jennifer Nash, for example, has called affect "an invitation to consider how structures of domination feel. . . . Simply naming structures fails to do justice to how they move against (and inside of) our bodies" (2019, 30). What Nash reminds us is that bodies are always more than *just* governed and that affect theory offers us a departure point distinct from biopolitics. *Biopolitics,* or the *biopolitical,* is a term coined by the French philosopher Michel Foucault. It references a shift in modes and means of power in the eighteenth and nineteenth centuries concerning the invention, management, and maintenance of the population. Here biopolitics draws attention to the ways that power is characterized through the care and maintenance of life and how power molds, contains, fosters, and regulates "life itself." Biopolitics is part of Foucault's broader concern over how power functions and how subjects of power—broadly conceived—are formed and governed (1978, 139–45).

A notion of biopolitics is central to much work in anthropology concerned with how the body occupies political imaginations and functions, how power works and flows across bodies in contemporary times, and how the body itself informs modalities of power. As Foucault writes, "The body is also directly involved in a political field; power relations have an immediate hold upon it; they invest it, mark it, train it, torture it, force it to carry out tasks, to perform ceremonies, to emit signs" (1995, 25).

For many contemporary anthropologists, attending to the body is part of a poststructuralist shift concerned with how subjects are formed and disciplined. An attention to biopolitics illuminates how even small and mundane forms of care—in all of its guises—over life is linked to projects of governance. The biopolitical is a concept deployed to think through these dynamic relations of care over life and death, vibrantly depicting how life itself has come to be managed by a range of actors generating new subjectivities and ways of being and relating.

Affect theory stretches and augments medical anthropology's long-standing commitment to the body, discourse, and discipline. As Kevin O'Neill writes, "In a biopolitical conception of the body, the body is largely understood as acted upon; these discursive analyses render the body limp. . . . This does not satisfy from the point of view of affect theory, as the body is—simply put—not always docile, but also excitable" (2015, 208).

15. On the interaction of affect, religion, and space, O'Neill writes, "Affect as a religiously managed and politically manipulated sensation makes legible a series of spaces that are not territorial but are nonetheless deeply political. These include, for example, the felt distance that exists between the pious and the impious" (2015, 209). As O'Neill continues, we encounter something similar in Elizabeth Povinelli's rendering of the "disjuncture between reason and affect." Referring to multicultural Australia, Povinelli writes on felt difference: "I should be tolerant, but you make me sick" (2002, 4). In turning to "affective space," O'Neill suggests we pay attention to the felt spaces that tie bodies together or set them apart. These are "moments when affect serves as the medium through which spatial divisions and interconnections become legible" (2013, 1103).

O'Neill's attention to the production of affective space reminds us that "a focus on the production of affective space prompts an interest in the politics of felt difference: between whiteness and the racialized other; between the saved and the sinner; between life and death . . . a politically charged spatial divide made legible through a visceral and deeply political kind of disgust" (2013, 1104). In other words, the body becomes the material on which spaces of religious difference—among multiple other kinds of difference—can be readily felt. I have elsewhere written about the notion of felt and cultivated salvific space, which I term the *salvific sensorium* (Denyer Willis 2018). The salvific sensorium is a kind of sensed space and territory that exists by engaging the senses with a divine alterity that reconfigures worth and temporal binds. It is affectively generative, if fleetingly so: an ephemeral emancipation from spaces of denigration and oppression.

16. One of the most compelling and still nagging questions that emerges in relation to religious media, however, is what Matthew Engelke calls a "problem of presence," meaning "how a religious subject defines and claims to construct a relationship with the divine through the investment of authority and meaning in certain words, actions and objects" (2007, 9). In Engelke's rich ethnographic work, he spends time with the Friday Apostolics at the Friday Masowe Church in Zimbabwe. His ethnography unfolds a fascinating and richly historical tale about how the Friday Apostolics came to understand the path to religious transcendence as *immaterial*. Eschewing the Bible itself, they strive to achieve a "live and direct" relationship with God. To make sense of this, Engelke weaves a history of Southern African colonialism and the power wielded by the written word of the Bible with a theoretically rich account of semiotics and religious materiality. In the end the immateriality of Friday Apostolics' faith is read as a tangibly material one, even if defined as immaterial.

Tracking Webb Keane (2003), Richard Parmentier (1994), and Charles Peirce (1955), Engelke suggests that semiotic forms such as the gestures, images, smells, objects, and more that communicate a message between the human and the divine are shown to be undeniably material and—of critical importance—"made, not given" (2007, 10). What Engelke demonstrates so well is that it is only through an attention to materiality—meaning an attention to everyday life and how history lives on and is made sense of—that anthropologists can understand how Christians deal with the uncertainty embedded in the problem of God's presence itself and the "stakes of [God's] absence" (13).

1. AVOWAL

1. In *Outlawed: Between Security and Rights in a Bolivian City*, Daniel Goldstein characterizes the state as an "absent presence" when describing the ways that police do their work in Bolivia (2012, 32). Here Goldstein is building on the work of Walter Benjamin, who describes policing's powers as a "nowhere tangible, all-pervasive, ghostly appearance in the life of civilized states" (2021, 48). Goldstein describes this as a form of governance that makes "the state into a phantom, at once there and not there, a ghostly presence that generates more insecurity than it prevents" (2012, 6).

Abandonment is another word used to describe this haunting: it is often described as the presence of the state felt *through its absence* (Daniel Goldstein 2016; Biehl 2005). A critique of the idea of abandonment, however, is that a place like the western *subúrbios* isn't really abandoned—that is, abandoned spaces are not separate from the rest of the city. It makes little sense to make distinctions between city and "slum," formal and informal, or *morro* (hill) and *asfalto* (pavement). There are capillary everyday connections between these urban realms that nullify the possibility of anything being truly abandoned. The fact that a place like Batan, for example, has always had "police" (whether drug traffickers, militia, or others) with clear relations to capital-P Police is illustrative of empirical interconnectedness.

Indeed, as Ananya Roy argues, if we insist that informality is the "habitus of the dispossessed" (2011, 233), we obscure how informality is a category imposition that both authorizes violence against the margins and constitutes the margins themselves (Das and Poole 2004). Or, as Bülent Diken has argued, Rio's favelas are not marginal but rather central to the logic of the city itself (2005). João Biehl's (2005) work and conception of abandonment grapples with this trouble between absence and presence as well. In *Vita: Life in a Zone of Social Abandonment,* Biehl further develops Orlando Patterson's (1982) concept of *social death* as an outcome of abandonment. In the reading of *Vita,* many have understood social death as an endpoint, or at least the second-to-last stop before an unmourned death.

In this way Biehl's social death and Giorgio Agamben's (1995) concept of "bare life" often get linked together, largely because both grapple with the problematic of "letting die." Biehl's use of social death as an endpoint, though, is thoroughly hesitant—he carefully proposes the term *"ex-human"* to capture "the difficult truth that these persons have been de facto terminally excluded from what counts as reality" (2005, 52). But he worries that by "representing the condition of the *abandonados* [the abandoned] through such a philosophical sounding term as ex-human, I might generate a distance and thus unintentionally participate in discursive regimes that ultimately miss the paradoxes and dynamism involved in letting the Other die" (317).

2. Almost all the Evangelical men I came to know well have had complicated histories of abuse as both perpetrators and victims of race-based violence, unemployment, and drug and alcohol use as well as trafficking. The research of Christina Vital da Cunha (2009a, 2009b) in Brazil shows the complex ways that Evangelicalism and drug trafficking are knotted together in the form of the "Evangelical drug dealer." This occurs through logics of future repentances and *also* modes of governance that make use of Evangelical codes of behavior and monetary donations.

This has also been central to prison logics, such as how conversion to Pentecostalism and neo-Pentecostalism has typically occurred within Laertius Costa Pellegrino, colloquially known as "Bangu 1," the maximum-security prison that sits at the center of Rio's western *subúrbios* (see Thompson [2022] for a discussion of Evangelicalism within Rio's penal system more broadly).

Conversion, here, is not used as a route out of drug trafficking but instead binds traffickers together in an even more selective protection group, as Brazil's prisons are notoriously dangerous and underserviced communities run by trafficking organizations themselves (King and Valencia 2014). At the same time, Enrique Desmond Arias (2014) has explored how militias are using Evangelical conversion to sway voters, underscoring the ways that (in)security, religion, and formal politics are intertwined.

3. This is broadly true of most forms of Pentecostal and Charismatic Christianity, not a peculiarity of Rio. As Manuel Vásquez argues, "this type of Christianity is often carried out by itinerant prophets, healers, and religious entrepreneurs who highlight the power of a Holy Spirit that knows no territorial boundaries. . . . Christianities animated by a deterritorializing and deterritorialized Holy Spirit seem to have the upper hand over locative Christian modes of dwelling. . . . [They] appear to have the creative adaptability to operate in multiple peripheries" (2011, 272). Indeed, the deterritorializing nature of Pentecostal and Charismatic Christianity more broadly produces a multiplicity of Pentecostalisms across a variety of locations that are, in fact, deeply territorialized, such that Pentecostal Churches are, as Joel Robbins explains, "effectively local regardless of their denominational embeddedness. . . . Churches are staffed from top to bottom with locals who constitute them as institutions responsive to local situations" (2004a, 127).

4. This is, of course, distinctive from how many conceptualize political possibility, rights, and citizenship in the Brazilian city (Holston 2008). Indeed, David Harvey explains how the city and a person are potentially transformed together: "The right to the city is far more than the individual liberty to access urban resources: it is a right to change ourselves by changing the city. It is, moreover, a common rather than an individual right since this transformation inevitably depends upon the exercise of a collective power to reshape the processes of urbanization. The freedom to make and remake our cities and ourselves is, I want to argue, one of the most precious yet most neglected of our human rights" (2008, 23). Here I track what happens when these prevailing logics of citizenship and right-based terrains of political engagement are reconfigured by an Evangelicalism that reframes experiences of state abandonment and subsumes any call for rights in the traditional or normative sense.

2. DISINFECTANT

1. Jennifer Roth-Gordon has examined how Brazilian racialized identities are made through a "sensory regime associated with whitening" (2013, 298;

see also Jacobs 2009). In Brazil notions of smell and race often work together in implicit and explicit ways. Patricia de Santana Pinho describes how the requirement to regulate "o cheiro negro" (2010, 108)—which Roth-Gordon translates as "black smell"—is an essential aspect of managing Blackness to demonstrate "proper bodily discipline" (2013, 298). Brazil is not unique in this way. Smell, in fact, often delineates difference. As Constance Classen (1992) argues, smell is a particularly insidious way to catalog the imposed boundaries of race, class, and morality. Or, as Martin Manalansan writes, "The sense of smell is the basis for recognition and misrecognition. . . . It provides an opportunity to affiliate, to belong as well as to disidentify and to ostracize" (2006, 44).

Perceptions of smell, especially of smells that supposedly do not belong, work alongside conceptions of whiteness and Blackness in stealthy ways. In a study on the antebellum US South, for example, Bridget Heneghan (2003) argues that even among the wealthy, white skin alone was not a reliable marker of racial purity or whiteness. The fulcrum of whiteness instead lay in a laborious care of the body and its things, such as tea sets and whitewashed walls. These white things served as extensions of the white body, and their care garnered whiteness.

In this way race was not just about skin color but a cultivated presentation of oneself and one's things. People particularly guarded against the risk of encountering contaminating smells in this context. Heneghan tracks how white slave owners wrote in contemporary periodicals about the best construction materials for housing slaves, arguing that framed timber was superior because logs absorbed the odor and the "stench and filth" of slaves, who filled cracks in log construction with stinking "dirty rags, old shoes, coon skins, chicken feathers." She also describes how southern homes were kept pure—read white—by segregating the odors of cooking from the main house (2003, 149, 150).

2. Janice Perlman describes how there were so many migrants arriving daily from the northeast that a whole new business venture of direct bus lines from the state of Paraiba in the northeast directly to City of God opened. While City of God was not the final destination point in itself, it was a handy jumping-off point to what was then Rio's "wild" west side (1976, 55–59).

3. In "Civilizing" Rio: Reform and Resistance in a Brazilian City, 1889–1930, Teresa A. Meade shows how from 1902 onward the explicit project of Rio's city officials was to move the undesirable working poor out of the city center into an expansive but contained suburban region, which could be held at arm's reach from the downtown Rio they envisioned as the home of an elite cosmopolitan population (1997, 74). One of the first goals of this cleansing project was the removal of cortiços from the city center. Cortiços were

tenement houses for the freed persons, rural migrants, immigrants, and enslaved peoples put out for hire who composed Rio's independent poor population. In her account of one of the first *cortiços* to be destroyed in Rio in the 1890s, Brodwyn Fischer (2008) explains how the racial prejudice that guided the anti-*cortiços* campaigns were founded on claims of hygiene. In the 1850s, in the name of preventing disease following a cholera outbreak, a new kind of expert emerged: the professional hygienist. Here, a notion of hygiene was used to denote a moral cleanliness as well.

Meade describes how in 1891 Dr. Agostinho José de Souza Lima, a public-health inspector, described the *cortiços* as lacking "moral virtue," marked by "sordid promiscuity" (1997, 69). Tasked with preventing further outbreaks, the newly formed Junta Central de Higiene Pública (Central Board of Public Hygiene) decided that *cortiços* represented a significant risk to a "civilized" Rio. The hygienist Cândido Barata Ribeiro, Rio's first prefect, or mayor, claimed in 1887 that *cortiços* fed "the lubricity of vice, which shamelessly flaunts itself, wounding the *eyes and ears* of serious society, and . . . also that ragged and repugnant misery, which makes of laziness a throne" (quoted in Fischer 2008, 33; emphasis added). It is surprising that he did not mention a wound to the nose as well, as subsequent depictions of Rio's favelas typically hinge on this too.

4. *Branqueamento* encapsulates a beauty project that goes far beyond physicality. It describes what it might mean to be *desirable* in a global ordering of bodies, streets, temporalities, and political imaginations, akin to what Roth-Gordon terms the "soft eugenics" that linger and discipline bodies in Rio (2013, 297). Alexander Edmonds's ethnographic work in Rio examines the ways that skin lighteners, hair straighteners, and cosmetic surgery offer an "alleviation of African traits," as though Blackness constituted a kind of public-health crisis: a sickness of space and the individual (2010, 161).

5. Indeed, none of this would be possible without the *medium* of the captured waste fragrance. "The media turn," Matthew Engelke explains, occurred as anthropologists and scholars of religion began to conceive of religion "as mediation" (2010, 371; see also Klassen 2007; Meyer 2004, 2006; Meyer and Moors 2005; Morgan 2008). They shifted their attention from debates over religious belief and practice (Asad 1983, 1993; Needham 1972; Ruel 1997), instead attuning to the things that make belief possible, be they cassette tapes (Hirschkind 2006); veils (Abu-Lughod [1986] 2016; Mahmood 2001); books (Engelke 2007); radio (Schulz 2006); or even dreams (Mittermaier 2010). Here media does not just mean a technology of communication but instead might best be conceived of as "middle grounds: something through which something else is communicated, presented, made known—whether that something is a book or a pair of eyes" (Engelke 2012, 227–28).

The "media" of religion is also often a commentary on modernity. E. B. Tylor's (1871) work on the anthropology of religion, which famously defined religion as "the belief in spiritual beings," is notable for situating religion as a belief system (i.e., not material) but, somewhat conversely, also for tying belief and materiality together. As Matthew Engelke (2012) explains, Tylor used the materiality of particular religions as a way to classify and place cultural groups on an evolutionary scale.

In Tylor's (1871) model there was a presumed correlation between a cultural group's civilization and the materiality of their spiritual beings. For the "rude races" spirits and souls could have a physical presence in the world, whereas for "civilized" Protestant Christians, whose religious beliefs stood at the pinnacle of his scale, God was always immaterial. Theirs was a religiosity that had stripped itself of so-called gratuitously barbaric materials—from altars to lingering ghosts. In this way, as Engelke notes, "immaterial religion, then, both as theoretical construct and as a moral norm, was a product of modernity" (2012, 211; see pages 210–12 for a robust analysis). As Engelke continues, an attention to materiality is an attention to lived experiences; it is a consideration of the politics and variations in time, place, bodies, movements, landscapes, and ecologies.

6. As Alain Corbin describes in his social life of smell in eighteenth- and nineteenth-century France, "The power of odors to stir the affective memory . . . the violent confrontation of the past and present engendered by recognition of an odor, could produce an encounter that, far from abolishing temporality, made the 'I' feel its own history and disclose it to itself" (1986, 82).

7. Amira Mittermaier's (2012) research on the material life of dreams in Cairo sensitively diverts the conversation on religious materiality and self-cultivation, as it has been explored by Saba Mahmood (2001) and Charles Hirschkind (2006). Exploring the divinely given dreams and visions of a Sufi community, Mittermaier begins to unpack what has been sacrificed by an attention to self-cultivation above most else in studies of Islam. In her study, where people are divinely acted on, she asks us to open ourselves to something beyond "this-worldly-oriented forms of religiosity" (2012, 252). In attuning herself to the act of being acted up, she is also attuning herself to an "ethics of passion" (249). Employing the concept of passion from Godfrey Lienhardt, who suggests that our understanding of the relationship between humans and the divine is limited by having "no word to indicate an opposite of 'actions' in relation to the human self" (1961, 151), Mittermaier takes an ethics of passion to be an ethics of relationality.

In this way an ethics of passion is about recognizing the ways that human ethics are always shared, entangled, and produced in relation to one another. Mittermaier argues that the divine dreams that her informants receive constitute relations with—and interventions by—"the Elsewhere." Advancing the work of Dipesh Chakrabarty (2000), Mittermaier uses the concept of "the Elsewhere" to capture the "realm of alterity that exceeds the visible social world" by refusing to bracket ghosts and spirits as "social constructs" (2012, 256). It also expands the range of characters who can act upon a person, stretching our notion of what kinds of structures and forces to include in our ethnographies that figure significantly in peoples' lives.

This work is part of a wider attention to the materiality of religious life within the anthropology of religion that has breathed new life into the concept of religious belief through the foregrounding of how everyday experiences come to constitute belief. *Belief* has long been understood as an inadequate term for conceptualizing religious phenomenon (Asad 1993; Lindquist and Coleman 2008; Needham 1972). A rigid concept of belief suggests an uncomfortable coherence of experiences across peoples and religious groups. It further simplifies—or sidesteps—the relationship between belief and ritual, at times making belief a purely functional actor with moral or explanatory power, with little—or too much—attention paid to the hierarchy or convergence between the two.

As Talal Asad's (1993) famous critique of Clifford Geertz (1966) makes clear, Geertz's singular attention to belief as an adherence to something that then *informs* experience ignores how practice, discourse and power—basically the ways that religious subjects are partly formed through their material circumstances—shape belief itself. "My argument," states Asad, "is not just that religious symbols are intimately linked to social life (and so change with it), or that they usually support dominant political power (and occasionally oppose it). It is that different kinds of practice and discourse are intrinsic to the field in which religious representations (like any representation) acquire their identity and their truthfulness" (1993, 122).

In this way a reified notion of belief constructs a binary between interiority and exteriority, with little attention to self-cultivation (Mahmood 2001; Hirschkind 2006) or the diverse ways that feeling (Tambiah 1985), aspiration, affect (O'Neill 2013, 2015), and the negotiations of these multiple frames shape lived experiences in ways at once practical and always entangled with symbolic and material experience that may have multiple and shifting valences. Steven Carlisle and Gregory Simon attempt to resolve the inadequacy of belief as an analytical vehicle by embracing the ways that people (to them "informants" or "subjects") still talk and use a notion of belief to explain their various commitments and faiths: "Our subjects also work through the problems of belief, both culturally and psychologically. Through their practices, discourses, and meditations, our subjects find ways to believe particular truths amid many possible truths, determine what it means to believe, conceive of the relationships between belief and practice, and assess the significance of belief for understanding the nature and moral status of human beings" (2012, 222). Thus, they argue that one way to "write against belief" (Lindquist and Coleman 2008) is to write instead about "believing selves" and their "subjective commitments to truths" that orient and shape "an individuals' subjective engagement with the world" (Carlisle and Simon 2012, 222–23).

Omri Elisha has written about the trouble with belief and the constitution of Pentecostal personhood, by shifting to a discussion about faith, intersubjectivity, and divine agency. He argues that we need to let go of the binary between something akin to faith—which encapsulates affect, trust, and feeling—and, on the other end, belief, as derived from intellect or cognitive conviction. For Elisha, whose work partly concerns receiving the gifts of God, specifically glossolalia, "Evangelical conceptions of faith highlight a process of transcendence that encompasses both emotion and propositional reasoning and consumes both body and mind, resulting in the 'birth' of a reconstituted, sanctified self." He adds the stipulation, however, that he first and foremost takes faith to be a "cultural construct, a category of Christian discourse and practice, and an object of Evangelical reification. . . . From this perspective, as an object of analysis, faith is hardly different from other useful yet empirically problematic categories within anthropology, including witchcraft, spirit possession, liminality and race" (2008, 59).

8. Mary Douglas has informed much work in the anthropology of waste. Dirt, for Douglas, is "matter of out of place," much the same way that a malodor is invoked as a disorder or a boundary violation (2002, 44). Dirt constructs and preserves notions of the self and the other, serving specific social, cultural, and political functions. But the actual waste or smell matters too. As Joshua Reno elaborates, waste is "more than a symptom of culture. . . . [It] is a material that has effects in the world, including local and global political disputes, liberal and illiberal forms of governance, competing assessments of economic and moral value, and concerns about environmental pollution and crisis" (2015, 558). Dirt is not just symbolic, then; it also moves and does things in the world.

Neoliberal structures and postcolonial topographies often—at least initially—dictate waste's circuits and its management, but waste seeps into places, creatively conjoining with the informality of the margins where trash becomes treasure. A central component in discard studies is the attention paid to people who perform waste labor and their creative work at turning waste or trash "into treasure" (Millar 2008, 25). In this way Evangelicals are certainly waste laborers of a certain kind, but, more than that, they trouble Douglas's (2002) category of matter out of place. As others have documented, while waste laborers understand waste as potential, waste still seems to belong *somewhere*. And this somewhere is often not centers but rather within "waste flows" that seem to travel in rather predictable ways: from centers to peripheries, following global capitalist circuits (Reno 2015, 564). Cruise ships dump their waste in Haiti, and landfills are displaced from urban Toronto to postindustrial Michigan, for example.

For Evangelicals in Rio's *subúrbios*, though, waste *is* in its place, for a different reason: it has been gifted and placed in Evangelical pathways to prosperity. This labor gives value, but this value, as Kathleen Millar points out, emerges from the painful paradox that precarious work actually *enables* people "to contend with insecurities in other dimensions of their lives" (2014, 34). Pentecostals mining the margins for prosperity constitute a form of optimism very much alert to harm in a city bent on pessimism toward them.

3. IN ATTENTION TO PAIN

1. Others have told me still even more versions of that day, saying that there was a *caveirão* but that the *caveirão* was just for show. A woman in her seventies said, "The *caveirão* was there just for fun: they were only 'capturing territory' from their own police friends," implying that on-duty police were simply assisting off-duty police (the militia). She didn't deny the *caveirão;* she just gave it yet another possible meaning. My neighbors, however, told yet another version: they said that a *caveirão*—labeled with the knife-through-a-skull insignia of the Batalhão de Operações Policiais Especiais—did drive into Batan; however, the men driving it and hanging from it were the militia members that BOPE was supposed to be "rescuing" them from.

These various narrations of what exactly happened, and whether that matters, and the so-called veracity of stories of violence have been taken up in detail by others, including Shoshana Felman and Dori Laub (1992) and Alessandro Portelli (1991). What is important to note from these works is how silences, (un)certain narratives, and (un)certain details are often organized by trauma; we should direct our attention to how official accounts get made and entrenched alongside felt and lived experiences that differ.

2. This type of abandonment is not new; it is an *economy of abandonment*, where abandonment functions as a specific kind of incorporation into the boundaries of the norm (Povinelli 2011). Abandonment is rarely final but is in fact a precarious *relation* itself. Ultimately, an attention to the relations of abandonment is crucial for complicating an atemporal notion of "let die" (Petryna and Follis 2015).

3. I follow ethnographers and theorists who foreground this materiality—where feelings, aesthetics, and sensory experiences are understood as

constitutive—while also carefully thinking through how the body is made and governed, without becoming a sort of second-string accounting (Ahmed 2010, 2017; Brennan 2004; Edu 2019; James 2010; Sedgwick 2003; Smith 2016).

4. WOLVES AT THE HEELS

1. Conditional cash transfers are a well-regarded highlight of social programming across Latin America. They are celebrated by the World Bank for providing "an entry point to reforming badly targeted subsidies and upgrading the equality of safety nets" (Fiszbein et al. 2009, 2). Brazil's Bolsa Família—one of the first and most lauded transfers in the region—has become an exemplar in the Global South more generally, held up not just as a way to eliminate poverty but as an instrument of social and economic citizenship. Women receive the money directly, on the conditions that they send their children to school and ensure they receive preventative health care, such as up-to-date vaccinations.

The Bolsa Família is often understood through the lens of a rights-based model of citizenship: as a way that citizenship is extended to the historically marginalized and poor. Conversely, it can also be seen as unintentionally consolidating historical systems of patronage and dependency. An ethnographic study by Gregory Duff Morton, for example, emphasizes that the Bolsa Família is not understood as a "right" but instead as a "social program" by many who receive it. Beneficiaries become "managers" of a benefit that can never be counted on, never demanded—only "managed" (2015, 1301).

Expanding on this creation of a manager subject position as opposed to a citizen position, Morton concludes that the "*Bolsa Família* rhetoric seems to bolster a political worldview in which there is a distinction between producing and managing. It may not be too much of a stretch to associate this worldview with the conception that left-wing political leaders have formed, in the past decades, about the state itself: the post-neoliberal state cannot produce, and hence leaves the creation of goods and services to the market. . . . The state's role, like that of the mother receiving *Bolsa Família*, is to manage the resources generated in the private sector" (2015, 1301).

2. In 2023 dollars R$1,000 would be roughly equivalent to earning US$300 per month. In 2012 this income of R$1,000 let their family of twelve scrape by: they didn't go hungry, and their self-built home could be maintained but not improved.

3. These deeply knowledgeable community-health agents, then, come to be seen as something akin to street-level bureaucrats in Brazil's expansive

but still deeply flawed public-health system. In the process of representing the public-health-care system, these community-health agents craft and reproduce notions of stateness and political subjectivity through surveilling individuals, and being seen daily, moving through communities in their canvassing vests.

4. Lula was a former laborer who rose to power through a powerful tide of workers' rights. Taking the presidency in 2002, he held power for eight years, bringing with him a renewed attention in Brazil to human rights, public health, decent living and working standards for the poor, and a range of much-lauded social programs premised on seeing people's livelihoods and futures improve over generations, through providing cash transfers, eradicating hunger, championing women's rights, and allowing access to universities for even the poorest citizens. When he left the presidency in 2010, he left as popular and beloved as he had ever been, famous and championed, both nationally and internationally, for ushering in what many regarded as a democratic and liberal Brazil.

Lula entrusted his legacy with his protégé, Dilma Rousseff, who was elected in the first election to follow Lula's two terms. Rousseff became the first woman to be president of Brazil. A former political dissident, imprisoned by the Brazilian dictatorship in the 1970s for two years, she exemplified the social and democratic ideals of the Workers' Party and Lula himself. In 2016, however, during a large-scale recession in the country, Rousseff was impeached on highly divisive charges that she had corrupted public accounts and broken budgetary laws. Her replacement was Michel Temer, a conservative who never became popular and was himself accused of corruption. As the 2018 election approached, the corruption scandal that had brought down Rousseff, colloquially known as the *lava jeto* (car-wash) scandal, led to charges being brought against Lula, who had been planning to run for president again, with polls showing him as the front-runner. In 2018 Lula was controversially jailed and prevented from mounting an election campaign.

Bolsonaro was elected in 2018 through a curious constellation of voters. On the one hand, the elite and middle classes, who had always disliked Lula and voted against the PT, threw their support behind Bolsonaro, seeing this as an opportunity to swing far away from the leftist leadership of the past two decades. But he was also supported by those in the poor suburban outskirts of cities like Rio and São Paulo, who now seemed to find the PT lacking, unlike poor voters in the northeast of the country, who had always represented the main voting bloc of the PT. While these parts of cities had been central to the elections of both Lula and Rousseff, these alliances appeared fragile in the election of Bolsonaro. In this void Bolsonaro emerged with a clear, though clearly unconventional, pathway to power (see French [2020]

for a richer history and a critical present-day evaluation of Lula and his political legacy).

This is the way the story is almost always narrated from the Center and
the Left: a theft of power premised on dubious corruption charges, buoyed
further by poor and duped Evangelical voters. But seeing this as purely aberration, as a momentary snap in voter attitudes, misses a more complex and
long-term landscape of voter fatigue with the Left and the kind of future that
was imagined in churches, through prayer and deep longing. This deep longing for a different kind of future was certainly manipulated, but it cannot be
ignored how deeply it was desired and felt: a future distinctive from one that
could be made through liberal political promise, it instead was premised in a
promise of salvation.

5. In *The Charismatic Gymnasium,* Maria José de Abreu is concerned
with the emergence of the Catholic Charismatic Renewal, tracking its growth
across two decades in Brazil. Charismatic Renewal is defined by distinctive
swings in politics, religion, and imaginations of what Brazil is, or could be.
Abreu attends to what she calls the "Charismatic gymnasium" as a way to
conceive of the materiality of Charismatics' aerobic prayer practices, pneu-
matic doctrine, and their adoption and transformation of mass media tech-
niques, along with the way they make use of tension in doctrine and bodily
discipline as operations of self and institution (2021, 4). In other words, tension is a form of power (6). As Abreu writes, "Much like the gymnast works
on stretching her limbs to the utmost limit so as to expose the network of the
joints and articulations of the body, Charismatics set to work on the elasticity that will bring the church back in form" (2).

Practice and doctrine combine into an operation both flexible and rigid,
where tension is about maintenance and preservation, but also always a *stretch:*
"It is an 'epic stretching,' in Brecht's words, the defining feature of which is precisely the ability to extend and bend to different traditions and protocols: a
propaedeutic of the gymnasium" (Maria Abreu 2021, 183). This discipline of
elasticity "functions as the adequate foundation of a particular power structure. The implicit aim of this structure is to produce religiously fluent bodies
concurrent with the rise of neoliberalism in Brazil" (2–3). Elasticity, as ever, is
a political, bodily, and moral venture; the practices of elasticity constitute the
politics of life itself in late liberal arrangements.

Indeed, this celebration of elasticity is of course due to its potential for the
elaboration of extremes, in politics, the body, space, aesthetics, even life. As
Maria Abreu explains, in flight, the gymnast is both air and ground, pushing
the human body to its extreme limits, even to the point that the gymnast
body itself often fails to thrive due to the intensity of elasticity demanded of
it. The gymnasium, an "impoverished" environment built only for this kind

of elasticity, with spectators and judges, is also consumed by it. In other words, "Impoverishment is two-fold: it *both* draws on a Christian tradition of self-effacing asceticism (*ascesis*, training) *and* approximates the latter to the powers of potentiality intrinsic to Brazil's socioeconomic and political era. Impoverishment, thus conceived, is not a status or an identity one can own or locate. It is power's own flexible expression: impoverishment not as a socioeconomic condition but as the condition of the socioeconomic" (7).

5. FAILURES AND DEMONS

1. Since as early as 2010, across the suburbs and beyond, Evangelical churches and pastors have been uniting with militia members and traffickers, constituting a pervasive conservative and pro-police politics, which were early iterations of the politics and partnerships that would lead to Bolsonaro's win. A cartoon that traveled across social media in Rio's south side jeers at these alliances: a stereotypical image of a drug trafficker is depicted evicting an elderly Candomblé practitioner from a favela, saying, "Leave this community in the name of Jesus." The cartoon jeers at the way Pentecostalism is being harnessed by traffickers (as well as militias) to prop up their systems of governance and to evict people who have been historically critical of their governance. This form of exclusion and violence against practitioners of Afro-Brazilian religions by trafficker-Evangelical networks has been well documented as forms of human rights violations (Boaz 2020).

2. The night of the demon-extraction ceremony that opens this chapter was April 4, 2015. This was the same night that Complexo do Alemão—a large complex of favelas in the north side of Rio, visible from the runway of the airport—staged a massive protest and mobilization. People took to the streets to protest the police shooting of a ten-year-old boy and four others earlier in the week. While the center of Rio, of which the complex was seen as being a part, was reeling in protests, the pastors in the west side never mentioned the shooting or the movements in the street.

Walking along the quiet streets of Batan after the service, I asked Jovina why Batan was quiet tonight: "Why aren't people protesting here?" Jovina answered easily, "Because the south side is dangerous and unsafe. Why would we protest here? Here we have God and militias." Put to use to serve particular ends, salvation—and the energy and magnetism that often accompany it—can congeal in any number of ways. In that evening what felt like a *whoosh* was also a hardening of conservative politics, alliances, and boundaries.

References

Abreu, Maria José de. 2021. *The Charismatic Gymnasium: Breath, Media, and Religious Revivalism in Contemporary Brazil.* Durham, NC: Duke University Press.

Abreu, Maurício de Almeida. 1987. *Evolução urbana do Rio de Janeiro.* Rio de Janeiro: IPLANRIO.

Abu-Lughod, Lila. (1986) 2016. *Veiled Sentiments: Honor and Poetry in a Bedouin Society.* Reprint, Oakland: University of California Press.

Agamben, Giorgio. 1995. *Homo Sacer: Sovereign Power and Bare Life.* Stanford, CA: Stanford University Press.

Ahmed, Sara. 2004. "Collective Feelings, or The Impressions Left by Others." *Theory, Culture and Society* 21 (2): 25–42.

———. 2007. "A Phenomenology of Whiteness." *Feminist Theory* 8 (2): 149–68.

———. 2010. *The Promise of Happiness.* Durham, NC: Duke University Press.

———. 2017. *Living a Feminist Life.* Durham, NC: Duke University Press.

Alexander, Michelle. 2010. *The New Jim Crow: Mass Incarceration in the Age of Colorblindness.* New York: New Press.

Alves, Dina. 2017. "Rés negras, juízes brancos: Uma análise da interseccionalidade de gênero, raça e classe na produção em uma prisão paulistano." *Ciências Sociais,* no. 21, 97–120.

Alves, Jaime Amparo. 2014. "Neither Humans nor Rights: Some Notes on the Double Negation of Black Life in Brazil." *Journal of Black Studies* 45 (2): 143–62.

———. 2018. *The Anti-Black City: Police Terror and Black Urban Life in Brazil.* Minneapolis: University of Minnesota Press.

Araújo, Fábio Alves. 2016. "'Não tem corpo, não tem crime': Notas socio-antropológicas sobre o ato de fazer desaparecer corpos." *Horizontes Antropológicos* 22 (46): 37–64.

Arias, Enrique Desmond. 2014. "Violence, Citizenship, and Religion in a Rio de Janeiro Favela." *Latin American Research Review* 49 (SI): 149–67.

Asad, Talal. 1983. "Anthropological Conceptions of Religion: Reflections on Geertz." *Man*, n.s., 18 (2): 237–59.

———. 1993. *Genealogies of Religion: Discipline and Reasons of Power in Christianity and Islam.* Baltimore: Johns Hopkins University Press.

Assembléia Legislativa do Estado do Rio de Janeiro. 2008. *Relatório Final da Comissão Parlamentar de Inquérito Destinada a Investigar a Ação de Milícias no Âmbito do Estado do Rio de Janeiro: Comissão Parlamentar de Inquérito.* Resolução No. 433/2008. https://pt.slideshare.net/lcazenha /relatrio-cpi-das-milcias.

Benjamin, Walter. 2021. *Toward the Critique of Violence: A Critical Edition.* Edited by Peter Fenves and Julia Ng. Palo Alto, CA: Stanford University Press.

Bento, Maria Aparecida Silva. 1995. "A mulher negra no mercado de trabalho." *Estudos Feministas* 3 (2): 479–87.

Berlant, Lauren. 2011. *Cruel Optimism.* Durham, NC: Duke University Press.

Bialecki, Jon. 2009. "Disjuncture, Continental Philosophy's New 'Political Paul,' and the Question of Progressive Christianity in a Southern California Third Wave Church." *American Ethnologist* 36 (1): 110–23.

———. 2017. *A Diagram for Fire: Miracles and Variation in an American Charismatic Movement.* Oakland: University of California Press.

Biehl, João. 2005. *Vita: Life in a Zone of Social Abandonment.* Berkeley: University of California Press.

Birman, Patricia, and David Lehmann. 1999. "Religion and the Media in a Battle for Ideological Hegemony: The Universal Church of the Kingdom of God and TV Globo in Brazil." *Bulletin of Latin American Research* 18 (2): 145–64.

Boaz, Daniel N. 2020. "'Spiritual Warfare' or 'Crimes against Humanity'? Evangelized Drug Traffickers and Violence against Afro-Brazilian Religions in Rio de Janeiro." *Religions* 11 (12): 1–18.

Brennan, Teresa. 2004. *The Transmission of Affect.* Ithaca, NY: Cornell University Press.

Burdick, John. 1993. *Looking for God in Brazil: The Progressive Catholic Church in Urban Brazil's Religious Arena.* Berkeley: University of California Press.

———. 1999. "What Is the Color of the Holy Spirit? Pentecostalism and Black Identity in Brazil." *Latin American Research Review* 34 (2): 109–31.

Butler, Judith. 2006. *Precarious Life: The Powers of Mourning and Violence.* London: Verso.

Caldeira, Teresa. 2000. *City of Walls: Crime, Segregation and Citizenship in São Paulo.* Berkeley: University of California Press.

Caldwell, Kia. 2003. "'Look at Her Hair': The Body Politics of Black Womanhood in Brazil." *Transforming Anthropology* 11 (2): 18–29.

———. 2007. *Negras in Brazil: Re-envisioning Black Women, Citizenship, and the Politics of Identity.* New Brunswick, NJ: Rutgers University Press.

Cano, Ignácio. 1997. *Letalidade da ação policial no Rio de Janeiro.* Rio de Janeiro: ISER.

———. 2010. "Racial Bias in Police Use of Lethal Force in Brazil." *Police Practice and Research: An International Journal* 11 (1): 31–43.

Cardoso, Francisco Paulino. 2017. "O fim de arco iris: Os desafios da luta antirracista no Brasil contemporâneo." *Pedagógica* 19 (40): 33–42.

Carlisle, Steven, and Gregory M. Simon. 2012. "Believing Selves: Negotiating Social and Psychological Experiences of Belief." *Ethos* 40 (3): 221–36.

Chakrabarty, Dipesh. 2000. *Rethinking Working-Class History: Bengal, 1890–1940.* Princeton, NJ: Princeton University Press.

Chalhoub, Sidney. 1988. "Medo branco de almas negras: Escarvos, libertos e republicanos na cidade de Rio." *Revista Brasileira de Historia* 8 (16): 83–105.

Chari, Sharad. 2017. "Detritus." *Somatosphere*, October 30, 2017. http://somatosphere.net/2017/10/detritus.html.

Classen, Constance. 1992. "The Odor of the Other: Olfactory Symbolism and Cultural Categories." *Ethos* 20 (2): 133–66.

———. 1998. *The Color of Angels: Cosmology, Gender, and the Aesthetic Imagination.* New York: Routledge.

Classen, Constance, David Howes, and Anthony Synnott. 1994. *Aroma: The Cultural History of Smell.* New York: Routledge.

Claudino, Nilton. 2011. "My Pain Doesn't Make the Papers." *Piaui* 59 (August). https://piaui.folha.uol.com.br/materia/my-pain-doesnt-make-the-papers/.

Coleman, Simon. 2000. *The Globalisation of Charismatic Christianity.* Cambridge: Cambridge University Press.

Comaroff, Jean, and John L. Comaroff. 1999. "Occult Economies and the Violence of Abstraction: Notes from the South African Postcolony." *American Ethnologist* 26 (2): 279–303.

———. 2000. "Millennial Capitalism: First Thoughts on a Second Coming." *Public Culture* 12 (2): 291–343.

Cook, Ian. 2004. "Follow the Thing: Papaya." *Antipode* 36 (4): 642–64.

Corbin, Alain. 1986. *The Foul and the Fragrant: Odor and the French Social Imagination.* Cambridge, MA: Harvard University Press.

Crawley, Ashon T. 2017. *Black Pentecostal Breath: The Aesthetics of Possibility.* New York: Fordham University Press.

Csordas, Thomas. 1993. "Somatic Modes of Attention." *Cultural Anthropology* 8 (2): 135–56.

Das, Veena, and Deborah Poole. 2004. *Anthropology in the Margins of the State.* Santa Fe, NM: School for Advanced Research Press.

Denyer Willis, Laurie. 2018. "It Smells Like 1,000 Angels Marching: The 'Salvific Sensorium' in Rio de Janeiro's Western *Subúrbios.*" *Cultural Anthropology* 33 (2): 324–48.

De Witte, Marleen. 2011. "Touched by the Spirit: Converting the Senses in a Ghanaian Charismatic Church." *Ethnos* 76 (4): 489–509.

Diken, Bülent. 2005. "City of God." *City* 9 (3): 307–20.

Douglas, Mary. 2002. *Purity and Danger: An Analysis of Concepts of Pollution and Taboo.* New York: Routledge.

Drabinski, John E. 2015. "James Baldwin's Afro-Optimism." Public lecture, Committee on Globalization and Social Change, Graduate Center, City University of New York, March 19, 2015.

Edmonds, Alexander. 2010. *Pretty Modern: Beauty, Sex, and Plastic Surgery in Brazil.* Durham, NC: Duke University Press.

Edu, Ugo Felicia. 2019. "Aesthetics Politics: Negotiations of Black Reproduction in Brazil." *Medical Anthropology* 38 (8): 680–94.

Edwards, Michael, and Méadhbh McIvor. 2022. "The Anthropology of Grace and the Grace of Anthropology." *Cambridge Journal of Anthropology* 40 (1): 1–17. https://doi:10.3167/cja.2022.400102.

Elisha, Omri. 2008. "Faith beyond Belief: Evangelical Protestant Conceptions of Faith and the Resonance of Anti-humanism." *Social Analysis* 52 (1): 56–78.

Engelke, Matthew. 2007. *A Problem of Presence: Beyond Scripture in an African Church.* Berkeley: University of California Press.

———. 2010. "Religion and the Media Turn: A Review Essay." *American Ethnologist* 37 (2): 371–79.

———. 2012. "Material Religion." In *The Cambridge Companion to Religious Studies,* edited by Robert A. Orsi, 209–29. Cambridge: Cambridge University Press.

Felman, Shoshana, and Dori Laub. 1992. *Testimony: Crises of Witnessing in Literature, Psychoanalysis, and History.* Routledge: Taylor and Francis.

Fernandes, Nelson da Nóbrega. 2011. *O rapto ideológico da categoria subúrbio.* Rio de Janeiro: Apicuri.

Ferreira da Silva, Denise. 2014. "Ninguém: Direito, racilidade e violéncia." *Revista Meritum* 9 (1): 67–117.

Fischer, Brodwyn M. 2008. *A Poverty of Rights: Citizenship and Inequality in Twentieth-Century Rio de Janeiro.* Palo Alto, CA: Stanford University Press.

Fiszbein, Ariel, Norbert Schady, Francisco H. G. Ferreira, Margaret Grosh, Niall Keleher, Pedro Olinto, and Emmanuel Skoufias. 2009. *Conditional*

Cash Transfers: Reducing Present and Future Poverty: Overview. Washington, DC: World Bank Group.

Flauzina, Ana Luisa, and João Helion Costa Vargas. 2017. *Motin: Horizontes de genocidio anti negro na diaspora.* Rio de Janeiro: Brado Negro.

Foucault, Michel. 1978. *The History of Sexuality: An Introduction.* Vol. 1, *The Will to Knowledge.* London: Penguin.

———. 1995. *Discipline and Punish: The Birth of the Prison.* New York: Vintage Books.

French, John D. 2020. *Lula and His Politics of Cunning: From Metalworker to President of Brazil.* Chapel Hill: University of North Carolina Press.

Freston, Paul. 1993. "Brother Votes for Brother: The New Politics of Protestantism in Brazil." In *Rethinking Protestantism in Latin America,* edited by Virginia Garrard-Burnett and David Stoll, 66–110. Philadelphia: Temple University Press.

———. 1995. "Pentecostalism in Brazil: A Brief History." *Religion* 25 (2): 119–33.

———. 2001. "The Transnationalization of Brazilian Pentecostalism: The Universal Church of the Kingdom of God." In *Between Babel and Pentecost: Transnational Pentecostalism in Africa and Latin America,* edited by Andre Corten and Ruth Marshall-Fratani, 196–215. Bloomington: University of Indiana Press.

Geertz, Clifford. 1966. "Religion as a Cultural System." In *Anthropological Approaches to the Study of Religion,* edited by Michael Banton, 1–46. London: Tavistock.

Gifford, Paul. 2004. *Ghana's New Christianity: Pentecostalism in a Globalizing African Economy.* Bloomington: Indiana University Press.

Goldstein, Daniel M. 2012. *Outlawed: Between Security and Rights in a Bolivian City.* Durham, NC: Duke University Press.

———. 2016. *Owners of the Sidewalk: Security and Survival in the Informal City.* Durham, NC: Duke University Press.

Goldstein, Donna M. 2003. *Laughter Out of Place: Race, Class, Violence, and Sexuality in a Rio Shantytown.* Berkeley: University of California Press.

Guimarães, Antonio Sérgio Alfredo. 2003. "Racial Insult in Brazil." *Discourse and Society* 14 (2): 133–51.

Hartman, Saidiya. 2007. *Lose Your Mother: A Journey along the Transatlantic Slave Route.* New York: Farrar, Straus and Giroux.

———. 2017. "The Terrible Beauty of the Slum." *Brick: A Literary Journal,* July 28, 2017. https://brickmag.com/the-terrible-beauty-of-the-slum/.

———. 2019. *Wayward Lives, Beautiful Experiments: Intimate Histories of Social Upheaval.* New York: Norton.

Harvey, David. 2008. "The Right to the City." *New Left Review* 53 (September–October): 23–40.

Haynes, Naomi. 2012. "Pentecostalism and the Morality of Money: Prosperity, Inequality, and Religious Sociality on the Zambian Copperbelt." *Journal of the Royal Anthropological Institute* 18 (1): 123–39.

———. 2013. "On the Potential and Problems of Pentecostal Exchange." *American Anthropologist* 115 (1): 85–95.

Heneghan, Bridget T. 2003. *Whitewashing America: Material Culture and Race in the Antebellum Imagination*. Jackson: University Press of Mississippi.

Hinz, Kristina, and Juliana Vinuto. 2022. "Police Soldiers, Elite Squads, and Militia: Militarized Masculinities and Public Security Discourses in Rio de Janeiro (1995–2018)." *International Feminist Journal of Politics* 24 (1): 63–86.

Hirschkind, Charles. 2006. *The Ethical Soundscape: Cassette Sermons and Islamic Counterpublics*. New York: Columbia University Press.

Holston, James. 2008. *Insurgent Citizenship: Disjunctions of Democracy and Modernity in Brazil*. Princeton, NJ: Princeton University Press.

Howes, David. 1991. *The Varieties of Sensory Experience: A Sourcebook in the Anthropology of the Senses*. Toronto: University of Toronto Press.

Htun, Mala. 2004. "From 'Racial Democracy' to Affirmative Action: Changing State Policy on Race in Brazil." *Latin American Research Review* 39 (1): 60–89.

Jacobs, Margaret D. 2009. *White Mother to a Dark Race: Settler Colonialism, Maternalism, and the Removal of Indigenous Children in the American West and Australia, 1880–1940*. Lincoln: University of Nebraska Press.

James, Erica Caple. 2010. *Democratic Insecurities, Violence, Trauma, and Intervention in Haiti*. Berkeley: University of California Press.

Keane, Webb. 2003. "Semiotics and the Social Analysis of Material Things." *Language and Communication* 23 (3): 409–25.

King, George, and Randy Valencia. 2014. "Environmental Risk and Well Integrity of Plugged and Abandoned Wells." In *Proceedings: SPE Annual Technical Conference and Exhibition*. Amsterdam: Society of Petroleum Engineers. http://dx.doi.org/10.2118/170949-MS.

Klassen, Pamela E. 2007. "Radio Mind: Protestant Experimentalists on the Frontiers of Healing." *Journal of the American Academy of Religion* 75 (3): 651–83.

Kramer, Eric W. 2005. "Spectacle and the Staging of Power in Brazilian Neo-Pentecostalism." *Latin American Perspectives* 32 (1): 95–120.

Lanz, Stephan. 2016. "The Born-Again Favela: The Urban Informality of Pentecostalism in Rio de Janeiro." *International Journal of Urban and Regional Research* 40 (3): 541–58.

Leeds, Anthony. 1974. "Housing Settlement Types, Arrangements for Living, Proletarianization, and the Social Structure of the City." *Latin American Urban Research* 4 (1): 67–99.

Lefebvre, Henri. 1996. *Writings on Cities*. Oxford: Wiley-Blackwell.

Lefèvre, Fernando. 1993. "Esta criança é um bandido! Este bandido é uma criança!" *Journal of Human Growth and Development* 3 (2): 57–60.

Lepselter, Susan. 2016. *The Resonance of Unseen Things*. Ann Arbor: University of Michigan Press.

Lienhardt, Godfrey. 1961. *Divinity and Experience: The Religion of the Dinka*. Oxford: Oxford University Press.

Lindquist, Galina, and Simon Coleman. 2008. "Against Belief?" *Social Analysis* 52 (1): 1–18.

Lorenzi, Lucia (@empathywarrior). 2021. "As I staked the soil for the peas this afternoon, I thought about how staking in academia is so often about defensiveness, about occupation." Twitter, April 15, 2021, 8:01 p.m. https://twitter.com/empathywarrior/status/1382846590562361345.

Luther, Martin. 1976. *Commentary on Romans*. Translated by J. T. Mueller. Grand Rapids: Kregel.

Machado, Maria das Dores Campos. 2005. "Representações e relações de gênero nos grupos Pentecostais." *Estudos Feministas* 13 (2): 387–96.

Mahmood, Saba. 2001. "Feminist Theory, Embodiment, and the Docile Agent: Some Reflections on the Egyptian Islamic Revival." *Cultural Anthropology* 16 (2): 202–36.

Manalansan, Martin F. 2006. "Immigrant Lives and the Politics of Olfaction in the Global City." In *The Smell Culture Reader*, edited by Jim Drobnick, 41–52. New York: Berg.

Mariz, C. L., and M. D. C. Machado. 1994. "Pentecostalismo e a redefinição do feminino." *Religião e Sociedade* 12 (1–2): 141–59.

Marshall, Ruth. 2009. *Political Spiritualities: The Pentecostal Revolution in Nigeria*. Chicago: University of Chicago Press.

Mbembe, Achille. 2001. *On the Postcolony*. Berkeley: University of California Press.

———. 2017. *Critique of Black Reason*. Translated by Lauren Dubois. Durham, NC: Duke University Press.

———. 2019. *Necropolitics*. Durham, NC: Duke University Press.

McCann, Bryan. 2014. *Hard Times in the Marvelous City: From Dictatorship to Democracy in the Favelas of Rio de Janeiro*. Durham, NC: Duke University Press.

Meade, Teresa. 1997. *"Civilizing" Rio: Reform and Resistance in a Brazilian City, 1889–1930*. University Park: Penn State University Press.

Meyer, Birgit. 2004. "Christianity in Africa: From African Independent to Pentecostal-Charismatic Churches." *Annual Review of Anthropology* 33:447–74.

———. 2006. "Religious Sensations: Why Media, Aesthetics and Power Matter in the Study of Contemporary Religion." In *Religion: Beyond a Concept*, edited by Hent de Vries, 704–23. New York: Fordham University Press.

Meyer, Birgit, and Annelies Moors. 2005. *Religion, Media, and the Public Sphere.* Bloomington: Indiana University Press.

Millar, Kathleen. 2008. "Making Trash into Treasure: Struggles for Autonomy on a Brazilian Garbage Dump." *Anthropology of Work Review* 29 (2): 25–34.

———. 2014. "The Precarious Present: Wageless Labor and Disrupted Life in Rio de Janeiro, Brazil." *Cultural Anthropology* 29 (1): 32–53.

Mittermaier, Amira. 2010. *Dreams That Matter: Egyptian Landscapes of the Imagination.* Berkeley: University of California Press.

———. 2012. "Dreams from Elsewhere: Muslim Subjectivities beyond the Trope of Self-Cultivation." *Journal of the Royal Anthropological Institute* 18 (2): 247–65.

Morgan, David. 2008. *Key Words in Religion, Media and Culture.* New York: Routledge.

Morton, Gregory Duff. 2015. "Managing Transience: Bolsa Família and Its Subjects in an MST Landless Settlement." *Journal of Peasant Studies* 42 (6): 1283–305.

Moyn, Samuel. 2010. *The Last Utopia.* Cambridge, MA: Harvard University Press.

Nash, Jennifer. 2019. *Black Feminism Reimagined after Intersectionality.* Durham, NC: Duke University Press.

Needham, Rodney. 1972. *Belief, Language, and Experience.* Chicago: University of Chicago Press.

Oliveira, Ney do Santos. 2007. "O caso do estado e as questões raciais, origem e caraterísticas sócio-econômicas de uma favela em niterói, estado de Rio de Janeiro." In *Espaço urbano e Afrodescendência: Estudos da espacialidade Negra urbana para o debate das políticas públicas,* edited by Henrique Rocha Ramos and Maria Estela Cunha, 137–54. Fortaleza: UFC.

O'Neill, Kevin Lewis. 2013. "Beyond Broken: Affective Spaces and the Study of American Religion." *Journal of the American Academy of Religion* 81 (4): 1093–116.

———. 2015. *Secure the Soul: Christian Piety and Gang Prevention in Guatemala.* Oakland: University of California Press.

———. 2017. "On Hunting." *Critical Inquiry* 43 (3): 697–718.

Oosterbaan, Martijn. 2006. "Divine Mediations: Pentecostalism, Politics and Mass Media in a Favela in Rio de Janeiro." PhD diss., University of Amsterdam.

Oro, Ari Pedro. 1997. "Neopentecostais e afro-brasileiros: Quem vencerá esta guerra?" *Debates do NER* 1 (1): 10–36.

Pallone, Simone. 2005. "Diferenciando subúrbio de periferia." *Ciência e Cultura* 57 (2): 11.

Pardue, Derek. 2010. "Making Territorial Claims: Brazilian Hip Hop and the Socio-geographical Dynamics of *Periferia*." *City and Society* 22 (1): 48–71.

Parmentier, Richard J. 1994. *Signs in Society: Studies in Semiotic Anthropology*. Bloomington: Indiana University Press.

Patterson, Orlando. 1982. *Slavery and Social Death*. Cambridge: Harvard University Press.

Peirce, Charles S. 1955. *Abduction and Induction: Philosophical Writings of Peirce*. New York: Dover.

Penglase, Ben. 2009. "States of Insecurity: Everyday Emergencies, Public Secrets, and Drug Trafficker Power in a Brazilian Favela." *PoLAR: Political and Legal Anthropology Review* 32 (1): 47–63.

———. 2011. "Lost Bullets: Fetishes of Urban Violence in Rio de Janeiro, Brazil." *Anthropological Quarterly* 84 (2): 411–38.

Perlman, Janice. 1976. *The Myth of Marginality: Urban Poverty and Politics in Rio de Janeiro*. Berkeley: University of California Press.

Perry, Keisha-Khan Y. 2013. *Black Women against the Land Grab: The Fight for Racial Justice in Brazil*. Minneapolis: University of Minnesota Press.

Petryna, Adriana, and Karolina Follis. 2015. "Risks of Citizenship and Fault Lines of Survival." *Annual Review of Anthropology* 44:401–17. https://doi.org/10.1146/annurev-anthro-102313-030329.

Pinho, Osmundo, and João Helion Costa Vargas. 2017. *Antinegritude: O impossivel sujeito negra na formação social brasileira*. Cachoeira: Editora da Universidade do Reconcavo Bahiano.

Pinho, Patricia de Santana. 2010. *Mama Africa: Reinventing Blackness in Bahia*. Durham, NC: Duke University Press.

Portelli, Alessandro. 1991. *The Death of Luigi Trastulli and Other Stories: Form and Meaning in Oral History*. Albany: State University of New York Press.

Povinelli, Elizabeth A. 2002. *The Cunning of Recognition: Indigenous Alterities and the Making of Australian Multiculturalism*. Durham, NC: Duke University Press.

———. 2011. *Economies of Abandonment: Social Belonging and Endurance in Late Liberalism*. Durham, NC: Duke University Press.

Reis, Vilma. 2005. "Na mira do racismo institucional: Quebrando o silêncio diante da matança em Salvador." *Irohin* 10 (11): 10–11.

Reno, Joshua. 2015. "Waste and Waste Management." *Annual Review of Anthropology* 44:557–72.

Robbins, Joel. 2003. "What Is a Christian? Notes toward an Anthropology of Christianity." *Religion* 33 (3): 191–99.

———. 2004a. *Becoming Sinners: Christianity and Moral Torment in a Papua New Guinea Society*. Berkeley: University of California Press.

———. 2004b. "The Globalization of Pentecostal and Charismatic Christianity." *Annual Review of Anthropology* 33:117–43.

———. 2009. "Pentecostal Networks and the Spirit of Globalization: On the Social Productivity of Ritual Forms." *Social Analysis* 53 (1): 55–66.

———. 2013. "Beyond the Suffering Subject: Toward an Anthropology of the Good." *Journal of the Royal Anthropological Institute* 19 (3): 447–62.

Robb Larkins, Erika. 2015. *The Spectacular Favela: Violence in Modern Brazil.* Oakland: University of California Press.

Rogers, Douglas. 2009. The Old Faith and the Russian Land: A Historical Ethnography of Ethics in the Urals. Ithaca, NY: Cornell University Press.

Roth-Gordon, Jennifer. 2008. "Conversational Sampling, Race Trafficking, and the Invocation of the Gueto in Brazilian Hip Hop." In *Global Linguistic Flows: Hip Hop Cultures, Youth Identities, and the Politics of Language,* edited by H. Samy Alim, Awad Ibrahim, and Alastair Pennycook, 63–77. New York: Routledge.

———. 2013. "Racial Malleability and the Sensory Regime of Politically Conscious Brazilian Hip Hop." *Journal of Latin American and Caribbean Anthropology* 18 (2): 294–313.

Roy, Ananya. 2011. "Slumdog Cities: Rethinking Subaltern Urbanism." *International Journal of Urban and Regional Research* 35 (2): 223–38.

Ruel, Malcolm. 1997. *Belief, Ritual and the Securing of Life: Reflective Essays on a Bantu Religion.* New York: Brill.

Rutherford, Danilyn. 2006. "Nationalism and Millenarianism in West Papua: Institutional Power, Interpretive Practice, and the Pursuit of Christian Truth." In *The Limits of Meaning: Case Studies in the Anthropology of Christianity,* edited by Matthew Engelke and Matt Thomlinson, 105–28. New York: Berghahn.

Salem, Thomas, and Erika Robb Larkins. 2021. "Violent Masculinities: Gendered Dynamics of Policing in Rio de Janeiro." *American Ethnologist: Journal of the American Ethnological Society* 48 (1): 65–79.

Samet, Robert. 2019. "The Subject of Wrongs: Crime, Populism, and Venezuela's Punitive Turn." *Cultural Anthropology* 34 (2): 272–98.

Scarry, Elaine. 1985. *The Body in Pain: The Making and Unmaking of the World.* Oxford: Oxford University Press.

Schulz, Dorothea E. 2006. "Promises of (Im)mediate Salvation: Islam, Broadcast Media, and the Remaking of Religious Experience in Mali." *American Ethnologist* 33 (2): 210–29.

Sedgwick, Eve Kosofsky. 2003. *Touching Feeling: Affect, Pedagogy, Performativity.* Durham, NC: Duke University Press.

Sexton, Jared. 2011. "The Social Life of Social Death: On Afro-Pessimism and Black Optimism." *InTensions* 5 (Fall–Winter): 1–47.

Shange, Savannah. 2019. *Progressive Dystopia: Abolition, Antiblackness, and Schooling in San Francisco.* Durham, NC: Duke University Press.

Shapiro, Nicholas. 2015. "Attuning to the Chemosphere: Domestic Formaldehyde, Bodily Reasoning, and the Chemical Sublime." *Cultural Anthropology* 30 (3): 368–93.

Sharpe, Christina. 2016. *In the Wake: On Blackness and Being.* Durham, NC: Duke University Press.

Simone, AbdouMaliq. 2019. *Improvised Lives: Rhythms of Endurance in an Urban South.* Cambridge: Polity.

Simpson, Audra. 2014. *Mohawk Interruptus: Political Life across the Borders of Settler States.* Durham, NC: Duke University Press.

Skidmore, Thomas E. 1999. *Brazil: Five Centuries of Change.* New York: Oxford University Press.

Smith, Christen A. 2016. *Afro-Paradise: Blackness, Violence, and Performance in Brazil.* Urbana: University of Illinois Press.

Sojoyner, Damien M. 2017. "Another Life Is Possible: Black Fugitivity and Enclosed Places." *Cultural Anthropology* 32 (4): 514–36.

Sousa Silva, Eliana. 2013. "Rifles: In Rio's City Center No, but in the Favela Yes?!" *RioOnWatch*, June 23, 2013. https://rioonwatch.org/?p = 9726.

Stevenson, Lisa. 2014. *Life beside Itself: Imagining Care in the Canadian Arctic.* Oakland: University of California Press.

Stewart, Kathleen. 2007. *Ordinary Affects.* Durham, NC: Duke University Press.

———. 2010. "Afterword: Worlding Refrains." In *The Affect Theory Reader,* edited by Melissa Gregg and Gregory J. Seigworth, 339–53. Durham, NC: Duke University Press.

Stoler, Ann Laura. 2016. *Duress: Imperial Durabilities in Our Times.* Durham, NC: Duke University Press.

Strhan, Anna. 2015. *Aliens and Strangers? The Struggle for Coherence in the Everyday Lives of Evangelicals.* New York: Oxford University Press.

Tambiah, Stanley Jeyaraja. 1985. *Culture, Thought, and Social Action: An Anthropological Perspective.* Cambridge, MA: Harvard University Press.

Thompson, David C. 2022. "Evangelical Christianity as Infrastructure in Brazil's Penal System." *Journal of Latin American Studies* 54 (3): 1–23.

Tsing, Anna Lowenhaupt. 2015. *The Mushroom at the End of the World: On the Possibility of Life in Capitalist Ruins.* Princeton, NJ: Princeton University Press.

Turra, Cleusa, and Gustavo Venturi. 1995. *Racismo cordial: A mais completa análise sobre o preconceito de cor no Brasil.* São Paulo: Atica.

Tylor, E. B. 1871. *Primitive Culture: Researches into the Development of Mythology, Philosophy, Religion, Art, and Custom.* Cambridge: Cambridge University Press.

Van Dijk, Teun A. 2009. *Society and Discourse: How Social Contexts Influence Text and Talk.* Cambridge: Cambridge University Press.

Vargas, João H. Costa. 2006. "When a Favela Dared to Become a Gated Condominium: The Politics of Race and Urban Space in Rio de Janeiro." *Latin American Perspectives* 33 (4): 49–81.

————. 2013. "Taking Back the Land: Police Operations and Sport Megaevents in Rio de Janeiro." *Souls* 15 (4): 275–303.

————. 2018. *The Denial of Anti-Blackness: Multiracial Redemption and Black Suffering*. Minneapolis: University of Minnesota Press.

Vásquez, Manuel. 2011. *More Than Belief: A Materialist Theory of Religion*. New York: Oxford University Press.

Vital da Cunha, Christina. 2009a. "Da Macumba às campanhas de cura e libertação: A fé dos traficantes de drogas em favelas no Rio de Janeiro" [From *Macumba* to liberating and curative campaigns: The faith of drug traffickers in Rio de Janeiro's favelas]. *Revista TOMO* 14 (January–June): 229–65.

————. 2009b. "Traficantes evangelicos: Novas formas de experimentação do sagrado em favelas cariocas" [Evangelical drug traffickers: New forms of experiencing the sacred in Rio de Janeiro's favelas]. Plural 15 (December): 23–46.

————. 2018. "Pentecostal Cultures in Urban Peripheries: A Socio-anthropological Analysis of Pentecostalism in Arts, Grammars, Crime and Morality." *Vibrant, Virtual Brazilian Anthropology* 15 (1). https://doi.org/10.1590/1809-43412017v15n1a401.

Weber, Max. 1905. *The Protestant Ethic and the "Spirit" of Capitalism and Other Writings*. London: Allen.

White, Mia C. 2018. "Rebellion and Theory of Love." Paper presented at Pembroke College, University of Cambridge, March 12, 2018.

Zaluar, Alba. 1994. *Condomínio do diabo*. Rio de Janeiro: Revan.

Index

abandonment: anti-Blackness, 66; bodies, 65; deflated, 106; economy of, 136n2; governance, 11, 65, 66; landscapes, 56; political, 117n1; practices of, 65; and precarity, 71; presence and absence of state, 128–129n1; relation of governance, 65–66; Rio, 40; salvation, 41; state, 21, 128n1, 130n4; violence, 21

Abreu, Maria José de, 85, 88, 139n5

Agamben, Giorgio, 129n1

Ahmed, Sara, 62, 116n1, 124n9

Alexander, Michelle, 121n6

Alves, Jaime, 6, 121–123n7

Amigos dos Amigos, 36

Ana, 1–2, 3, 8–10, 11, 12, 15, 80–81, 95

angels: Ana, 1–2, 3, 8, 9, 10–11, 15; believing in, 20; calling on, 33; and demons, 76, 112, 113; moving among us, 75; prayer circle, 28, 31, 32; presence of, 18; talking to, 16

anti-Blackness, 18, 61, 66, 72, 79

anti-LGBTQ legislation, 110

Arias, Enrique Desmond, 130n2

Asad, Talal, 134n7

Batan: Ana, 8–9; author living in, 34–35, 36, 90, 113; boulder, 24; changing, 84;

church services, 39; community of, 60; drug-trafficking, 100; Evangelicalism in, 7, 12, 20, 38, 85; governance, 100–101; location, 3–4; pacification, 62–63, 65, 66; place of God, 25; police, 129n1; quiet streets, 140n2; residents' stories, 117n2; state violence, 5–6

Berlant, Lauren, 116n1

Biehl, João, 65, 129n1

Blackness, 87

bodies: abandonment, 65; accommodating rhythms, 65; bearing pain, 59, 61–62, 71, 74; bending, 68; Black, 62, 121n6; children's, 29; demons, 98; endurance, 11; ethnographies of, 72; exterminations, 6; feeling God in, 109; feeling in, 3; felt spaces that tie bodies together, 127n15; governance, 70–71, 124n9; 126n14; importance of, 61; love for, 70; moving, 67; moving through space, 19–20; moving through the world, 116–117n1; power relations, 73; prayer, 75–76, 97; religiously fluent, 139n5; sensory life of, 16, 19; shifting, 116n1; soft eugenics, 132n4; tattoos, 34, 111; touch, 69, 70; women's, 29, 61, 62

Bolsa Família: cash-transfer program, 80,
137n1; distrust in, 86; rejecting, 80–84
Bolsonaro, Jair, 7–8, 22, 85–86, 110, 138n4

Caldwell, Kia, 62
Carlisle, Steven, 134n7
Cesarean incision, 58, 59, 67, 70
Chakrabarty, Dipesh, 134n7
Chari, Sharad, 117n1
The Charismatic Gymnasium, 139n5
chemical waste, 57
churches: Catholic, 38; Christian Church, 53;
Danilo, 104; Evangelical, 3, 10, 38, 55,
82–83, 95–97, 114, 118n3, 140n1;
Good Friday, 93–94; João Vitor, 36;
Jovina, 105; Megan's death, 33, 34; Nina,
31; Pentecostal, 38, 80, 130n3; Protes-
tant Church, 56; raised in, 15; roadside,
21; services, 39, 77, 86; small, 111; and
voters, 139n4
citizenship, 22, 62, 84, 111–112, 130n4,
137n1
*"Civilizing" Rio: Reform and Resistance in a
Brazilian City, 1889–1930*, 131n3
Classen, Constance, 53, 131n1
Claudia, 67
Comaroff, Jean, 124n8
Comaroff, John, 124n8
Corbin, Alain, 133n6
Crawley, Ashon, 13, 17, 125–126n11
crentes (believers), 38
Csordas, Thomas, 72

da Cunha, Christina Vital, 129n2
Danilo, 99–100, 101–104
da Silva, Denise Ferreira, 6
da Silva, Luiz Inácio Lula, 85
demons: believing in, 20; bodies, 98; demon-
extraction ceremony, 140n2; Elisa and
Danilo, 101; exorcisms, 39; and grace,
22, 106; hunt for, 16; Jovina, 105; and
pastor, 97–98; prayer, 118n3; real, 22;
Rio, 112; spiritual combat with, 118n3;
symbolic, 22; and Vandila, 75–76
de Witte, Marleen, 70
Diana, 91
Diken, Bülent, 129n1
disinfectant: Ana, 10, 80–81, 95; author
helping make, 114; crafted from chemical
waste, 57; Milene, 42–44, 45, 50–53,
80–81, 113–114; politics of disinfectant,
49
dono da favela (favela boss), 100

Douglas, Mary, 135n8
Drabinski, John, 79

Edwards, Michael, 125n10
Elisa: bedridden, 31–32, 99; crib, 32–33;
Danilo, 99–101, 102, 104; doctors'
blame for Megan's death, 27; prayer, 28,
30–32, 33, 86–87; premature labor,
26–27; rumors about, 99–101, 102; second pregnancy, 84; tattoo, 33–34; Vila
Vintém, 100–101
Elisha, Omri, 135n7
Engelke, Matthew, 53, 128n16, 132n5
Enzo, 43, 44, 45–46, 48, 51–52, 81
ethnography, 20, 112
Evangelicalism: affirms life, 13; defining *subúrbios*, 22; and drug trafficking, 129n2;
embodied, 18; experience of, 116n1; fascist rule, 110; feeling emancipated, 11; in
Latin America, 36–37, 38, 56, 70, 111,
126n12; makes people feel worthy, 3;
more in *subúrbios* than center, 14; and
pain, 61; politics of worth, 72; and right-
wing politics, 13, 17; role of state, 2; state
abandonment, 130n4; transcends electoral politics, 7; and violence, 7, 8, 20
Evangelical podcasts, 20
Evangelicals: author's associates, 77; callings,
15–16; demons, 22; faith, 3; forms of conservatism, 22; God, 40; grace, 12, 13, 15,
16, 56, 109; identify as, 38; mistrust of
political Left and Right, 7; not dependent
on state, 14; periphery, 110; political
promise, 83; prayer, 41; refusal, 84; relationships to divine and city, 21; religious
feeling, 23; routes out of systemic injustice,
2; sanctity of fragrance, 53; state destruction, 40–41, 81–82; and state promises,
17; supporting Bolsonaro, 7, 85; trauma
and pain, 94; on Vila Vintém, 101; violence of, 7; waste laborers, 135–136n8
Evangelicals living in *subúrbios:* Ana, 1; fervor, 20; imagining in different ways,
13–14, 56, 111; not in periphery, 110;
pathways to prosperity, 136n8; politics of
grace, 109; state as "dangerous," 81; violent whims of state, 7
Evangelicos (Evangelicals), 38

Facebook church services, 20
Facebook Messenger, 90
favelas: beaches, 4, 62; Black communities,
47; *dono da favela* (favela boss), 100;

Founded in 1893,
UNIVERSITY OF CALIFORNIA PRESS
publishes bold, progressive books and journals
on topics in the arts, humanities, social sciences,
and natural sciences—with a focus on social
justice issues—that inspire thought and action
among readers worldwide.

The UC PRESS FOUNDATION
raises funds to uphold the press's vital role
as an independent, nonprofit publisher, and
receives philanthropic support from a wide
range of individuals and institutions—and from
committed readers like you. To learn more, visit
ucpress.edu/supportus.